A TWENTIETH-CENTURY COSMOS

The New Plan and the Origins of General Education at Chicago

INTRODUCTION

T he condition of the liberal arts at elite colleges has been highly visible in public discussions in the last several years, inspiring commentary in the press and on college campuses across the country. Some of this debate has come in response to issues of academic freedom, as colleges face criticism for failing to defend the rights of faculty to teach freely without political interference, as well as coercive pressures from outside the academy or from various interest groups within the campuses themselves (including, unfortunately, student groups seeking to pressure the faculty to teach or not teach in certain ways). Other voices have addressed the perceived failure of institutions to develop coherent and thoughtful curricular programs that enable students to engage the full sweep of liberal-arts disciplines. Among the latter are analysts who argue that elite institutions, under the sway of educational neoliberalism, have reduced the value of the liberal arts to their economic utility. Where higher education once sought the formation of character and intellectual autonomy, it has now conformed to the language and values of the marketplace. This, the

This essay was originally presented as the Annual Report to the Faculty of the College on October 31, 2006. John W. Boyer is the Martin A. Ryerson Distinguished Service Professor in History and the College, and Dean of the College.

argument goes, is perilous to the work of self-discovery, especially to the study of the humanities, which are being eclipsed by more lucrative majors in the STEM fields and economics. This is a potent and in some ways arresting argument. Yet it recapitulates many of the charges of educational corruption that have surfaced regularly about American higher education since the early twentieth century. It supposes an institution whose curriculum and mission are shapelessly adapted to new fads, lacking the legitimacy of a campus culture that is itself suffused with scholarly values.

Fortunately, that institution is not the University of Chicago. One of the defining themes of our 125-year history has been thoughtful curricular innovation by the faculty, rooted in the values of interdisciplinary thought, rigorous meritocracy, and intellectual analysis. These values lie at the heart of the Core, which introduces every student, regardless of major, to the practices of humanistic reflection as a basis for further study and has been able to accommodate many challenges since the 1930s.

The College's Core curriculum has been one the most effective instruments for our University to sustain our collective memory work. A curriculum is more than a set of formal prescriptions and requirements. It is a statement of basic values and a way by which the faculty can assert what is educationally important and what is not, and how it wishes to organize its own work, based on past traditions and past experience. The curriculum also comes to constitute the cognitive framework through which our alumni remember their intellectual accomplishments while on campus, giving them a special sense of having lived and been transformed in a special place. And our curriculum is a public commitment and a public affirmation that we will educate our students for the kind of future—humane, tolerant, enlightened—that all of us esteem and hope will always come to pass.

Since the early 1930s the College's curriculum has been most noted
for its tradition of general education. This year—2017–18—is the nine-
tieth anniversary of the formulation of the first plan to develop a program
of general education at the University of Chicago, a plan that led three
years later to the launching of the first Core courses in the College in the
autumn quarter of 1931. It is thus an appropriate moment to pause and
consider what these courses were, how they came about, how they embedded themselves in our institutional consciousness, and how they managed
to sustain themselves or their offspring in the decades that followed. A
few years ago Arnold Rampersad of Stanford University, who once taught
at Columbia University, observed that the Core curricula of universities
like Columbia and Chicago were like the federal interstate highway
system—you could never build them the same way again, but since they
exist, you can take care of them, keep them functioning, and help them
to achieve the educational objectives that are rather unique to such special
systems of liberal education.[1] In this essay I want to explore how that
"highway system" came to be built, who built it, why they built it, and
what we should do with it now.

1. See Charles McGrath, "What Every Student Should Know," *New York Times*,
January 8, 2006, http://www.nytimes.com/2006/01/08/education/edlife/what-
every-student-should-know.html. I issued an earlier version of this essay in
October 2006. The present version, completed in July 2017, offers a significant
revision which takes the story down to the present. I am extremely grateful to
Daniel Koehler and Michael Jones for their assistance. I am also grateful to Leon
Botstein, Terry N. Clark, Martin Feder, Hanna Holborn Gray, Paul H. Jordan,
Ralph Lerner, Joel Snyder, and William Veeder for answering questions about
specific individuals or events that are discussed in this essay.

Chauncey S. Boucher, undated photograph by Norman F. Maclean

THE NEW PLAN AND THE CREATION OF A GENERAL-EDUCATION PROGRAM

 ur traditions of general education date back to the late 1920s, when a group of colleagues at Chicago decided to revolutionize the world of higher education by creating what was called the New Plan, a bold attempt to synthesize broad fields of knowledge in an explicitly interdisciplinary framework for first- and second-year students in the College. The New Plan was our first Core curriculum, and the current curriculum, passed in 1998, owes much to the spirit and practices of the New Plan.

The New Plan was the brain child of Dean of the College Chauncey S. Boucher who was first appointed to the deanship in 1926. Briefly, during the late 1920s Boucher came to be dissatisfied both with the level of intellectual accomplishment of undergraduates at Chicago and with the somewhat lackadaisical way in which the University treated undergraduate education. Even before Robert Maynard Hutchins assumed the presidency in the summer of 1929 Boucher had conducted a lobbying campaign to create a new curriculum of general-education courses based on a comprehensive examination system and a new approach to undergraduate education.[2] Boucher argued:

2. See Chauncey S. Boucher, "Suggestions for a Reorganization of Our Work in the Colleges, and a Restatement of Our Requirements for the Bachelor's Degree," December 1927, Dean of the College Records, 1923–1958, box 27, folder 6; and "Report of the Senate Committee on the Undergraduate Colleges," May 7, 1928, ibid., folder 7, Special Collections Research Center, University of Chicago Joseph Regenstein Library. Unless otherwise noted, all archival documents cited in this essay are located in the center.

A trick of fate put me into the Dean's office where I soon began to get a much broader and entirely new perspective. At first I thought that a dean must necessarily spend most of his time and efforts quibbling with students over one or another of the numerous book-keeping regulations for the attainment of a degree, and on disciplinary problems—in fact I thought that a dean must be pri-marily a petty police officer, spending his time catching and torturing flies. I had no stomach for such activities any longer than was necessary to allow the President's office time enough to enlist a man to take the place. Very soon, however, I learned that Presi-dent Mason and Vice President Woodward were anxious to do something really significant with the Colleges and were ready to entertain any constructive suggestions which the Dean might have to offer. I then began in earnest to study the biggest problems of college education, particularly our own problems, and, by spend-ing as little time as possible on the petty affairs of the office, I soon became deeply interested in the major problem.[3]

Boucher's real ambition, articulated in many position papers that he wrote between 1927 and 1930, was to begin to recruit more motivated and academically gifted students to the Colleges and then to put them in a more coherent and rigorous instructional program that was not controlled by the departments and that would be protected by an inde-pendent Office of the Examiner. He sought to construct a *completely new system* of general education for all areas of the arts and sciences at the

---

3. Boucher, "Suggestions for a Reorganization of Our Work in the Colleges," 53–54. Boucher gave this long appeal to Max Mason in January 1928 and sent it to his colleagues in the University Senate on March 12, 1928.

University of Chicago, and he had to do so in a way that the influential factions of senior natural- and social-science faculty at Chicago would accept, if not actively embrace.

Having been inspired by a talk that President Max Mason gave to the Institute for Administrative Offices of Institutions of Higher Education in July 1927, Boucher began to survey the state of collegiate education nationally and to consult with experts who would speak with him:

I read more widely whatever literature would give me the current practice and progressive thought of men in other institutions; I talked with about thirty individuals in various departments and schools of the University of Chicago; in January 1928 I made a trip to learn first hand what is going on at Princeton, Columbia, and Harvard. I talked with many of the leading constructive thinkers at each of these institutions. My object was first of all to see what features of the practice at each of these institutions could be adapted to our conditions; secondly, I was anxious, if given any encouragement, to tell the main features of the plan on which I was to work, in order to get the constructive and corrective suggestion of these men whose training and experiences would make their opinions valuable.[4]

4. Boucher, "Suggestions for a Reorganization of Our Work in the Colleges," 51–52.

Boucher's visit to Columbia doubtlessly led him to investigate the Contemporary Civilization course first launched in 1919.[5] But it would be a mistake to think that Boucher was trying to copy such models, for the political and intellectual challenge that he faced at Chicago was much more radical than anything that the Columbia humanists like John J. Coss and Harry J. Carman had faced in the 1920s in creating their new history course. The relative prestige of the senior social, biological, and physical scientists among the arts and science faculty at Chicago at the time meant that Boucher had to attract their support and design a curriculum with a substantial investment in the natural and social sciences, along with the humanities. A critical turning point seems to have been his six-hour visit in New York City in late January 1928 with William S. Learned, a senior staff member at the Carnegie Foundation for the Advancement of Teaching and a remarkable interwar critic of secondary and tertiary levels of education in America. In 1927 Learned had published a tough critique of the state of American higher education in which he denounced "the bane of the average" that afflicted American colleges and universities. Looking over the landscape of college and university programs, Learned saw incoherence, lack of rigor, a jumble of course credits and grading practices that had no rational purpose or aim, and, most seriously, a complete distain for "the intellectual vision, energy, and

5. See John J. Coss, "A Report of the Columbia Experiment with the Course on Contemporary Civilization," in *The Junior College Curriculum*, ed. William S. Gray (Chicago, 1929), 133–46; Justus Buchler, "Reconstruction in the Liberal Arts," in *A History of Columbia College on Morningside*, ed. Dwight C. Miner (New York, 1954), 48–135; Gary E. Miller, *The Meaning of General Education: The Emergence of a Curriculum Paradigm* (New York, 1988), 35–41; and Timothy P. Cross, *An Oasis of Order: The Core Curriculum at Columbia College* (New York, 1995).

enthusiasm of young minds."[6] Boucher was much taken by Learned's proposals for enhancing curricular rigor and his disdain for course credits, and Learned encouraged him to pursue a set of fundamental, transdisciplinary structural reforms.[7] If any single outside influence shaped the creation of Chicago's first Core curriculum, it was the work of empiricists like William Learned and his colleagues at the Carnegie Foundation.[8]

A month later Boucher constituted and chaired a faculty committee that formulated his reform program and presented it to the University

6. William S. Learned, *The Quality of the Educational Process in America and in Europe* (New York, 1927), 42–48, 98–125. Learned was chiefly responsible for organizing the famous Pennsylvania Study which examined learning outcomes for large numbers of high school and college students in that state between 1928 and 1932 on the basis of systematic assessment testing. He was also the architect of the first Graduate Record Examination, created in 1937 on a trial basis with the cooperation of Harvard, Yale, Princeton, and Columbia.

7. Boucher reported that he considered Learned "to be the one man in the country, if there is any such one man, best prepared and best qualified to give a critical judgment on any such plan as the one proposed." After going over his plan with Learned, he was pleased to report that Learned "sincerely hoped the University of Chicago would adopt the plan and carry it into successful operation in the immediate future,...because if the University of Chicago were to inaugurate such a system of work and requirements, it would be more significant in its effects on both secondary and college education in this country than if it were done by any other institution." Boucher, "Suggestions for a Reorganization of Our Work in the Colleges," 52–53. On Learned's opposition to course-based credit and grading, see Paul F. Douglass, *Teaching for Self Education—As a Life Goal* (New York, 1960), 82–89. See also Ellen Condliffe Lagemann, *Private Power for the Public Good: A History of the Carnegie Foundation for the Advancement of Teaching* (Middletown, Conn., 1983), 101–7.

8. In his 1932 Inglis Lecture at Harvard, Learned spoke approvingly of "the recent revolution at the University of Chicago," signified by its use of new comprehensive examinations. See *Realism in American Education* (Cambridge, Mass., 1932), 27–28.

Senate on May 7, 1928. The committee was dominated by a centrist group of scholars who were sympathetic to the cause of undergraduate education. They included Julius Stieglitz, Anton Carlson, Leon Marshall, and, perhaps most notably, Charles Judd of the Department of Education. Boucher's plan called for a set of bold changes: the establishment of a junior-college program that would have its own curricular structure distinct from the control of the departments but taught by the regular research faculty; the revision of the curriculum for the first two years of the undergraduate work, which would replace ad hoc departmental offerings with broad survey courses based on research findings of the faculty (an idea that built on an earlier experiment in the natural sciences in the mid-1920s); the use of five general-education competency examinations to assess and evaluate student progress, which students might take whenever they felt ready; additional new subject area courses designed to meet student interest in early specialization, particularly in the natural sciences; and the abolition of mandatory quarterly course examinations.[9] Nor did Boucher restrict himself to intrepid curricular changes, for his plan also presumed that several million new dollars would be invested in new residence halls, in additional endowment to pay for the upkeep of these halls, and in the construction of instructional facilities and the expansion of undergraduate library resources as well.[10] Finally, although he insisted on

9. "Report of the Senate Committee on the Undergraduate Colleges (presented to the University Senate, May 7, 1928)," Presidents' Papers, 1925–1945, box 19. This report contains as well a "Supplementary Statement" by Boucher. The May 1928 report was based on a long document that Boucher prepared in December 1927, "Suggestions for a Reorganization of Our Work in the Colleges, and a Restatement of Our Requirements for the Bachelor's Degree."

10. "Suggestions for a Reorganization of Our Work," 53–58; as well as "Bait, cut by C. S. Boucher," January 7, 1930, 18–19, Presidents' Papers, 1925–1945, box 19. In mid-December 1928 the university announced a $2 million gift from

new resources for the College, Boucher wished to keep most of the actual instruction on the main quadrangles to avoid creating an undergraduate ghetto. For those who sought to marginalize undergraduate education at the University of Chicago, these proposals, taken in their entirety, were a declaration of war.

Boucher draped his plan in the aura of the research university with the research-based content of courses; the intellectual individualism, stamina, and autonomy required of undergraduates; and the regime of "scientific" testing that would evaluate student achievement. Among his original recommendations in May 1928 was the idea that the College should make it possible "to save time for the better students, who are able to develop themselves both faster and more thoroughly than the average student, by awarding the [bachelor's] degree on the basis of demonstrated accomplishment, rather than on a required number of course credits, and thus break up the lock-step system."[11] Boucher was convinced that he had designed a system that would eliminate most of the glaring ills that Learned found evident in American higher education. But he also hoped that, in attracting more intellectually independent students who would merit the respect and admiration of the regular departmental faculties, he would be able to rescue the undergraduate program at Chicago from its politically marginal status.

Boucher's strategy for a curricular revolution stumbled in early May 1928 when President Max Mason unexpectedly resigned to become

Julius Rosenwald (matched by a $3 million commitment from the university) for the construction of new undergraduate dormitories for men and women. "Proposal for a Dormitory Development on a 40% Gift and 60% Investment Basis," [1928], Records of the Department of Buildings and Grounds, 1892–1932, box 12.

11. "Supplementary Statement," May 7, 1928, 1, 11.

director of the Natural Sciences Division at the Rockefeller Foundation, with the informal understanding that he would then become president of the foundation within a year or two. The resulting power vacuum in the summer of 1928 put Boucher's scheme in limbo. Attempts to implement the reforms in a piecemeal fashion in later 1928 inevitably stalled, and Boucher felt isolated and unsupported, beset by powerful forces intent on thwarting his plans to strengthen undergraduate education.[12]

Still, Boucher was convinced that a more challenging and more imaginative curriculum would attract intellectually stronger students to Chicago, and he was prepared to gamble that the University could find ways to enhance student quality and commitment. Even though Chicago might lose a significant share of its weaker and less committed students, they would soon be replaced by

a better type of student; the young people of the United States are keen enough to recognize the best to be had in education quite as quickly or even more quickly than in any other line, and are interested enough in their own welfare and development to seek the best wherever it is to be found; therefore, these Eastern men [scholars with whom Boucher had consulted] predicted, if Chicago

12. The plan that Boucher brought before the University Senate was not a formal legislative proposal for that body, but rather a series of recommendations that would have to be considered first by the Faculty of the Colleges of Arts, Literature, and Science. This faculty met on May 15, 1928, and agreed to create two boards—one for the junior-college curriculum and one for the senior-college curriculum—to evaluate Boucher's proposals and then report back to the full faculty. The boards began to meet in the autumn quarter of 1928, but it soon became apparent that, lacking the presence of the new (and, as of yet, unnamed) president, it would be difficult to establish sufficient political consensus as to how to proceed.

were to adopt such a plan as here outlined, it would at once be recognized the country over as a performance superior to the old stereotyped and almost universal plan, and in a short time Chicago would have more applicants of better quality than ever before.[13]

For his basic instructional model Boucher adapted and expanded the structural idea of an interdisciplinary, trans-departmental "survey course" for freshmen in the natural sciences, entitled The Nature of the World and Man, that H. H. Newman and others in Biology had organized for sixty students each year beginning in 1924. This course, whose major organizing theme was the trajectory of human evolution, was taught on a two-quarter cycle, and by 1928 had 240 students. The Newman course aimed "to make clear the fact that all science is one and that there are no hard and fast lines between its various branches." Newman and his colleagues, who included Rollin T. Chamberlin, Anton J. Carlson, Harvey B. Lemon, Merle Coulter, Fay-Cooper Cole, Julius Stieglitz, Charles H. Judd, and others, had the striking goal in mind of presenting students with "a general philosophic view that will rationalize all of the order and unity in the natural universe."[14] Boucher used this course as a template for his larger and more ambitious plans to restructure the undergraduate curriculum as a whole.[15]

13. Boucher, "Supplementary Statement," May 1, 1928, 16, ibid.

14. H. H. Newman, The Nature of the World and of Man, Dean of the College Records, 1923–1958, box 5, folder 4. In 1926 Newman also published a formidable 550-page book, bringing together essays of sixteen collaborators who taught in the course, entitled The Nature of the World and of Man (Chicago, 1926).

15. Chauncey S. Boucher, The Chicago College Plan (Chicago, 1935), 17.

A crucial turning point that put Boucher's efforts back on track toward stunning success came in the summer of 1929, when the young Yale Law School dean, Robert Maynard Hutchins, assumed the presidency of the University of Chicago. Immediately after Hutchins's appointment was announced in April 1929, Boucher wrote two back-to-back letters to him, duly praising his appointment but also informing and lobbying Hutchins about his (Boucher's) plans. Boucher noted: "After a year of uncertainty, with the consideration of important questions of basic policy necessarily postponed, the election of anybody as president at this time would have given us a feeling of relief. But, your acceptance of the presidency has given us genuine satisfaction and has inspired us anew with enthusiasm and confidence." For Boucher "the most important project in educational policy which was before us for consideration when President Mason's resignation was announced is set forth in the report of the Senate Committee on the Undergraduate Colleges, dated May 1, 1928."[16]

Boucher proved to be an able advocate, and Hutchins slowly came to embrace the basic substance of Boucher's plan. Thus did Boucher gain a powerful ally who, as the new executive leader with the sovereign force of the presidency behind him, had the political resources and the moral authority to force Boucher's schemes through the faculty. Once Hutchins had determined in the autumn of 1930 to restructure the University to create four separate graduate divisions, it became logical to create an administratively separate college as well.[17] Boucher's conceptual ideas on a new curriculum for such a college and Hutchins's structural reforms

16. Boucher to Hutchins, April 27, 1929, and May 3, 1929, Dean of the College Records, 1923–1958, box 1.

17. See John W. Boyer, *The Organization of the College and the Divisions in the 1920s and 1930s* (Chicago, 2002), 10-64.

converged, and beginning in late December 1930 Boucher chaired an ad
hoc curriculum committee which crafted, over the course of two months,
a curriculum for the College whose centerpiece was a set of four year-long
general-education survey courses, with an additional survey in English
composition.[18] The new survey courses were to be administered by clus-
ters of faculty drawn from the four divisions, but under the administrative
and curricular aegis of the separate College.[19] Originally, Boucher
intended that most of the faculty participating in the College would have
simultaneous departmental memberships. It is of great importance to
remember that Boucher had no intention of creating a faculty separate
from and in opposition to the departments and the divisions. The University Senate concurred in this view when it authorized the College in
1932 to hire faculty members who did not have departmental memberships, but cautioned, "it is considered desirable that a large proportion of
the College faculty be members of Departments and Divisional faculties."[20]

Boucher was well aware that the audience for his new program consisted of many students who sought careers in the professions or in

18. The committee solicited reactions from the faculty and received a number
of thoughtful commentaries in late January 1931, which are filed in the Presidents' Papers, 1925–1945, box 19, folder 9. The final proposal, dated February
7, 1931, is in ibid., folder 8. Hutchins followed the work of the committee
closely, and met with them at least twice to discuss their progress.

19. See Chauncey S. Boucher, "Procedures to Put the Plan into Operation,"
November 1930, Dean of the College Records, 1923–1958, box 10, folder 2. A
convenient overview of the actual plan is offered by "First Year of New Plan in
the College," ibid. See also Boucher to Hutchins, October 16, 1930, with a
memo on "The College Curriculum," Presidents' Papers, 1925–1945, box 19,
folder 7.

20. "Minutes of the University Senate," November 19, 1932.

business and not in academic life.[21] Hence he tried to make his vision appealing to a broad range of students, stressing the timeliness and functional utility of a general-education program for students who wished to undertake careers in business, law, and medicine. Boucher insisted that "general education provides the basis for an intelligent discharge of these larger responsibilities which inevitably come to the man or woman who is really successful in a profession or vocation." But even for those who did desire academic careers general education was vital, since "the specialist in any field should be characterized by the wealth of his knowledge of many fields. To be only an expert results in a one-sided personality and limited usefulness."[22] All of this was to connect the New Plan to the world and to emphasize its relevance for professional careers outside as well as inside of the academy.

After securing the approval of the new curriculum by a vote of 65 to 24 at a general meeting of the Faculty of the College in early March 1931, and after conferring with the newly appointed divisional deans and with key department chairmen, Chauncey Boucher set out to organize four planning groups to create the new survey courses. The groups worked quickly and assembled necessary course materials, which Boucher found

21. See Chauncey S. Boucher, *The New College Plan of the University of Chicago* (Chicago, 1930), 5–6, 9, 14. A survey undertaken in 1932 of prospective student careers found that 27 percent of the male students intended careers in law, 20 percent in medicine, and 16 percent in business, advertising, or engineering. Seven percent intended careers in teaching, and 17 percent in science, with 5 percent wanting careers in journalism. See Robert C. Woellner, "The Selection of Vocations by the 1932 Freshmen of the University of Chicago," Dean of the College Records, 1923–1958, box 6, folder 6.

22. "Education and Careers" (Chicago, n.d.), 1. The pamphlet is unsigned, but was clearly by Boucher or under his direction.

the funds to purchase. Each course produced a detailed syllabus, which included a prose outline of the major arguments and material of the course together with detailed bibliographical citations for further reading. Substantial investments in books and equipment had to be made. Boucher also held several meetings in the spring of 1931 where all staff leaders met jointly to work out logistical and scheduling issues. Slowly, the appearance of a unified curriculum emerged. A key feature of the new general-education curriculum was that it would not depend on course grades but on six-hour final comprehensive exams administered by an independent Office of the Examiner, headed by Professor Louis L. Thurstone, a distinguished psychologist who did pioneering research in psychometrics and psychophysics. Students could pace themselves through the curriculum, taking the final comprehensives whenever they felt prepared to do so. The idea of individual agency, cast as the autonomy of student freedom, was a central feature of the logic of the New Plan.[23]

Attendance at the general-education survey courses was not mandatory to prepare for the comprehensive exams, although in most cases most students seem to have attended the course lectures. Students could register either for audit or for advisory grades, and most of the courses offered quarterly exams, papers, and quizzes that were intended to serve an advisory function, allowing a student to measure his or her progress within the course. The advisory grades did not convey graduation credit, however, since the comprehensive exams were the basis of receiving the

23. For the history of the Board of Examinations, see Benjamin S. Bloom, "Changing Conceptions of Examining at the University of Chicago," in *Evaluation in General Education*, ed. Paul L. Dressel (Dubuque, Iowa, 1954), 297–321.

College's certificate.[24] Grades were thus used only as advisory instruments, or to facilitate transfer credit if a student opted to move to another college.

THE BIOLOGICAL SCIENCES AND PHYSICAL SCIENCES GENERAL COURSES

I n the natural sciences Boucher had the advantage of being able to drawn upon a group of men who had already participated in The Nature of the World and Man course. The world of the natural sciences at Chicago in the late 1920s was exciting and filled with ambitious scholars, optimistic about the progress of their disciplines and certain that the new knowledge of modern science could be made both appealing to and relevant for a general undergraduate audience. The primary architect of the Biology course was Merle C. Coulter from the Department of Botany. Coulter was the son of John M. Coulter, the founder of modern botany at Chicago, with whom the younger Coulter had collaborated in writing a book defending modern evolutionary theories in 1926.[25] He was a product of Chicago, having received his undergraduate degree in 1914 and his PhD in 1919. As a young assistant professor Merle Coulter had

24. "The marks made in the comprehensive examinations, and not the quarterly reports, constitute the final record for purposes of fulfilling College requirements, awarding scholarships and honors, and fulfilling requirements for admission to a Division." A. J. Brumbaugh to M. C. Coulter et al., October 15, 1936, Dean of the College Records, 1923–1958, box 6, folder 9.

25. John M. Coulter and Merle C. Coulter, *Where Evolution and Religion Meet* (New York, 1926).

been a collaborator in The Nature of the World and Man, preparing a chapter of the textbook that accompanied that course. In 1930 he was an associate professor of botany, a man of considerable diplomatic skill, and an inspiring teacher. He did not enjoy the research reputation of his father, which he always regretted, but the General Biology course enabled him to make a significant professional contribution at the University.[26] When Chauncey Boucher asked him to lead the planning effort to get the new sequence off the ground, Coulter was eager to do so.

Coulter organized a course that depended on the cooperation of a number of other senior biologists, each of whom agreed to give several lectures in the course. He was assisted in his lectures by a team of younger biologists, including Alfred E. Emerson and Ralph Buchsbaum from Zoology and Ralph W. Gerard from Physiology, several of whom would go on to distinguished scholarly careers in the Division of the Biological Sciences. More senior members were also invited to give lectures, including Warder C. Allee, Fay-Cooper Cole, Lester R. Dragstedt, and Alfred S. Romer, with perhaps the most notable scholar being A. J. Carlson, popularly known as Ajax Carlson, a distinguished physiologist who gave fifteen lectures during the academic year and became one of the most beloved general-education faculty teachers in the College before World

26. Joseph Schwab later argued that Coulter had always stood in the shadow of his father, and his participation in the Biology course offered him a way to compensate for this situation: "He felt he should have been what his father had been, a research man. He kept up with the literature in the field, he read, he always had a rapport with the papers that were being printed and published and so on....Anyway, he had a research ideal which he did not fulfill." Interview of Joseph J. Schwab with Christopher Kimball, April 7, 1987, 59–60, Oral History Program.

War II.[27] Born in Sweden, Carlson came to America at the age of sixteen in 1891 knowing not a word of English. He worked as a carpenter's apprentice and planned on becoming Lutheran minister. But he soon became interested in physiology and ended up at Stanford, where he took a PhD in 1902. In 1904 Harper hired him as an instructor at Chicago, and by 1914 he was a full professor of physiology. Carlson was legendary for asking his students in his heavy Swedish accent the formidable question: "What is the evidence?" That students were often befuddled and even terrified as to how to answer Carlson's questions seemed to make him all the more appealing as a lecturer. Joseph Schwab remembered him as someone who "took no nonsense, he didn't talk professorese, he was a toughie."[28] Edwin P. Jordan, a former student who became the director of education at the Cleveland Clinic, recalled that "in creating a state of mind of skepticism, coupled with a desire to learn more, but to do this only on the basis of the scientific method, you have surely had an enormous influence not only on those who were directly touched by your teaching and investigative methods but also on their students and their students' students as well."[29] Merle Coulter later observed of Carlson's role in the Biological Sciences general course, "you were usually our chief offensive threat and a tower of strength on defense."[30] That a scholar of Carlson's stature was steadily devoted to the Biological Sciences general course as a matter of professional responsibility made its success all the

27. Lester R. Dragstedt, "Anton Julius Carlson, January 29, 1875–September 2, 1956," *Biographical Memoirs of the National Academy of Sciences* 35 (1961): 1–32; and idem, "An American by Choice: A Story about Dr. A. J. Carlson," *Perspectives in Biology and Medicine* 7 (1984): 145–58.

28. Interview of Joseph J. Schwab with Christopher Kimball, April 7, 1987, 34.

29. Jordan to Carlson, December 28, 1949, Anton J. Carlson Papers, box 1.

30. Coulter to Carlson, January 29, 1950, ibid.

Merle C. Coulter, undated

easier. But Carlson's ferocious empiricism and confident assaying of "the facts" of any intellectual problem was to become a subject of a campus-wide debate in 1934.

Merle Coulter was particularly proud that students would encounter "the most distinguished authority" in a specific field, thereby enabling the course to generate a "real 'University tone'" by giving first- and second-year students "contact with many of the most outstanding men on our University faculty."[31] In addition to the formal lectures students participated in weekly discussion conferences and also had access to what Coulter called "laboratory exhibits." Attendance at the latter was optional,

31. Merle Coulter, "Report on Ten Years of Experience with the Introductory General Course in the Biological Sciences," October 1941, 8, Dean of the College Records, 1923–1958, box 5, folder 8.

but Coulter reported in 1935 that "most of the students of previous years have attended regularly and have found these exhibits to be one of the most interesting and valuable parts of the course."[32]

Coulter's group crafted their outline, in considerable detail, during the spring of 1931. The course was intended to help cultivate "the scientific attitude of mind" among students by exposing them to various examples of the application of the scientific methods, to provide a level of basic knowledge of biology as would be needed by "a modern citizen," and to encourage among students an interest in "the grand machinery of the organic world and in the major concepts of biology." The course was divided into four major parts: a survey of the plant and animal kingdoms; an analysis of the dynamics of living organisms, including physiology and psychology; studies in evolution, heredity, and eugenics, and a section on ecology; and the adaptation of living organisms to their environment and to each other.[33] The autumn quarter focused on giving the student an evolutionary portrait of the organic world, moving from the plant kingdom to invertebrate and vertebrate animals to the most complex animal, the human being. The winter quarter then focused directly on the nature of human life, with lectures on blood, heart, respiration, digestion, enzymes, the kidneys and endocrine glands, the nervous system, nutrition, bacteria, and disease. The final part of the course related man to the world around him, using ecology and evolution as its central focus. Here the students heard lectures on evolution, heredity, mutation, eugenics, and ecology.

The course gained a strong coherence by its focus on the major concepts of evolution, structure, and function within the domain of biological

32. "General Introductory Course in Biological Science: Schedule of Conferences and Lectures, Autumn, 1935," ibid., box 6, folder 9.

33. "The General Course in Biological Science," [1931], ibid.

phenomena. Its inductive and experimental approach and its frequent invocation of the physical and chemical basis of human life and of the chemical and physical knowledge required to understand such processes as photosynthesis and respiration or the functioning of the nervous system afforded the course natural links to the material covered in the Physical Sciences general course. Coulter felt that it was especially valuable

> to give the student an understanding of and a respect for the unbiased method of thinking that characterizes, or should characterize, workers in the field of natural science....We hoped to drill the student in such a manner to improve his ability to think scientifically and/or strengthen his habit of thinking in this way. Recognizing that other courses on our campus would be aiming at the same general objective, we felt it appropriate for our course to stress that particular tool of the scientific method which modern biology cherishes most highly—controlled experimentation.[34]

Coulter's emphasis on the virtues of the scientific method, as customary and conventional as it might seem to us today, was in fact a decision of great curricular import, for it set the New Plan in a skills-oriented direction that transcended the conveying of raw data and factual information. It confirmed the excitement and prestige of science in the interwar period.

The course used a range of review materials, quizzes, and papers to achieve these noble ends, although these were only advisory and not for credit. In addition to the lectures and discussion conferences Coulter also organized each week an optional laboratory demonstration. Students were not permitted to handle specimens or equipment, so their role was

34. Coulter, "Report on Ten Years of Experience with the Introductory General Course in the Biological Sciences," 2.

to be one of the interested observer, not an active participant. Coulter actually believed that this was a more effective pedagogical approach since "more than once it has been remarked by adult visitors to some of our laboratory demonstrations that a half-hour of this type of thing is more valuable to the average student than a month of old-fashioned laboratory work." In 1934 Coulter estimated that between 60 and 70 percent of the students regularly attended the laboratory demonstrations.[35]

Coulter and his colleagues also pioneered the production of a series of short motion pictures with ERPI Classroom Films that provided demonstrations of experiments on such topic as the Heart and Circulation, Mechanisms for Breathing, Digestion of Foods, the Work of the Kidneys, the Endocrine Glands, the Nervous System, and Heredity. By 1940 eleven such films had been produced, and Coulter was proud that all of them were "good and some of them are remarkably good." The films were designed so that they appealed to more general audiences beyond university students, enabling viewers to see and understand complex biological processes "even more clearly than if they had been present in the laboratory." Coulter also admitted, "for better or worse, most of our young American students like the movies and are stimulated to an increased interest in biology by an occasional movie presentation."[36]

Among College students the Biological Sciences general course quickly became the most popular of the four general-education courses, and its coherent organization, overarching themes, and logical rhythm certainly contributed to that state of affairs. But there was also the quiet certainty

35. Statement by Merle Coulter, September 14, 1934, Dean of the College Records, 1923–1958, box 6, folder 9.

36. Coulter, "Report on Ten Years of Experience with the Introductory General Course in the Biological Sciences," 18–19.

and confidence that the course was genuinely important for young students, not only as citizens but as inhabitants of a closely and intimately shared natural world. Anton Carlson was particularly insistent: "the understanding of the physical man himself and his environment, the adjustment to and the control of his environment cannot be foreign to genuine liberal education."[37]

The parallel course in the physical sciences was organized by Harvey B. Lemon, a physicist who completed his undergraduate studies at Chicago (BA, 1906) and who had studied with Albert A. Michelson and Henry Gale at Chicago for the doctorate, completing a dissertation on spectroscopic studies of hydrogen in 1912. Lemon was interested in pedagogy, and authored several articles in the 1920s on the use of intelligence tests to diagnose the capability of students to succeed in science courses.[38] Lemon was a scholar of wide-ranging interests with a flair for the dramatic. He was also deeply committed to improving the teaching of physics, and from 1937–39 served as the president of the American Association of Physics Teachers. He also exercised stringent standards in the hiring of course assistants, noting that if one specific graduate student did not conduct himself in a "thoroughly dignified and grown-up fashion," he would "find himself demoted to the laboratory."[39]

37. Anton J. Carlson, "The Offerings and Facilities in the Natural Sciences in the Liberal Arts Colleges," *The North Central Association Quarterly* 18 (1943): 162.

38. Harvey B. Lemon, "Forecasting Failures in College Classes," *The School Review* 30 (1922): 382–87; idem, "Preliminary Intelligence Testing in the Department of Physics, University of Chicago," *School Science and Mathematics* 20 (1920): 226–31.

39. Lemon to Gale, June 6, 1936, Department of Physics Records, 1937–2002, box 9, folder 17.

Lemon was joined in the course by a distinguished chemist, Hermann Schlesinger, who had also received both his BA and PhD degrees at the University of Chicago, studying with Julius Stieglitz. Schlesinger joined the faculty in 1910 and was promoted to full professor in 1922; he eventually won the Priestly Medal of the American Chemical Society. Others who gave lectures included Gilbert A. Bliss, Otto Struve, Arthur H. Compton, William Bartky, J. Harlen Bretz, and other distinguished scholars, thus giving young College students a chance to encounter prominent scholars from across the division.[40]

The new course sought to integrate astronomy, mathematics, physics, chemistry, and geology into one year-long survey. It started with the earth as an astronomical body, considering the structure of the universe, the nature of planets and stars and their evolutionary origins; it continued with a survey of essential components of the physical sciences, beginning with the fundamental laws of energy, heat, and temperature as manifestations of atomic and molecular motions, and the nature of electricity, sound, light, and X-rays as examples of the phenomena of waves; and it continued with a study of basic chemistry, chemical elements, compounds, mixtures, solutions, and colloids; it followed with atomic weights and numbers, chemical transformations, the periodic system, chemical reactions, the atmosphere, ionization, and carbon compounds; and the course concluded with a study of the geological features of the earth, rocks, minerals, the formation of the mountains and oceans, climatic changes, and fossils as a geological record of life.

Both the Biological Sciences and Physical Sciences general courses were organized in a lecture-discussion format, having three lectures plus

40. A detailed history of the course is provided by Thornton W. Page in "The Two-Year Program: Physical Sciences," November 1949, Presidents' Papers, 1946–1950, box 12, folder 5.

one discussion a week. Both courses styled themselves as "state of the
art" in scholarly terms, and both profited from that crescendo of self-
confidence about the importance of the natural sciences to human life
that enveloped American research universities after World War I. The
war had given American scientists powerful opportunities to demonstrate the practical impact of modern science, not only for human
destruction but also for human regeneration and reconciliation. On our
campus, for example, Julius Stieglitz, the chair of Chemistry, who participated in the development of The Nature of the World and Man
course, was a bold and articulate spokesman for the view that chemistry
was a crucial partner for modern medicine and modern pharmacology:
"chemistry is the fundamental science of the transformation of matter,
and the transformation of matter almost at will obviously has inherent
in itself the realization of unlimited possibilities for good."[41] Stieglitz
was also a strong advocate of integrating the intellectual standards associated with advanced scientific research and graduate education into the
undergraduate curriculum. He was convinced that the University of
Chicago should

> develop to the utmost its singular opportunity for the most inspir-
> ing type of college education, resulting from the co-existence in a
> single institution of great graduate departments and great colleges
> crowded with eager thousands—the red blood of universities....
> Situated in the heart of the American nation, why should it hesitate
> to try the experiment of giving to its four years of college life every
> last ounce of benefit from the presence of its great graduate faculties
> and, reciprocally, of increasing the strength and research output of

41. Julius Stieglitz, *Chemistry in the Service of Man* (Chicago, 1925), 9.

its graduate schools in the manning of its college chairs and thus develop to the utmost the *American university*.[42]

Equally noteworthy was the greater sense of interdependence of various disciplines in the natural sciences, and the need for close collaboration across the disciplines to attain path-breaking conceptual and empirical discoveries. A proposal by Ezra J. Kraus of the Department of Botany in late 1927 to create an interdisciplinary Institute of Biology insisted that "the [fundamental biological] problems, rather than the departments of the university should serve as points of attack. Thus the work of perhaps several men in various departments could be coordinated and focused on a problem."[43] Vice President Frederic Woodward said that Kraus was "a great believer in cooperative research," and was "struck by the similarity of the situation in the biological and social sciences. He made a great impression on me and I think we should encourage him and back him up at every possible point."[44] As a young physicist writing in the early 1920s, Harvey Lemon was equally confident that science was on the threshold of enormous changes that educated men and women must understand, if only to prevent the kind of misuse of science that had (to his mind) taken place between 1914 and 1918:

Clear heads and sober minds are needed, as never before, to watch lest the genie prove to be an evil one providing us with the weapons

42. Julius Stieglitz, "The Past and the Present," *The University of Chicago Magazine*, March 1929, 233–39, here 239.

43. Kraus to Max Mason, October 24, 1927, "Institute of Biology," Presidents' Papers, 1889–1925, box 101, folder 1.

44. Woodward to Mason, August 29, 1927, ibid.

for our own destruction. The dreams of Jules Verne that fired the imagination of our boyhood, incredible as they then appeared, are today in many instances accomplished facts....As individuals in social and political life, we must keep pace with science; and, taking the warning from the fate of [Henry] Moseley, prevent the repetition of another such orgy of destruction as that which recently was detonated by the monumental stupidity of our so-called civilization.[45]

Lemon later insisted that science was not simply about generating ever more remarkable technical applications:

Applications of science have not been, and never will be, the chief motive of the scientific investigator or student. The study of pure science will never be abandoned as long as human beings are characterized by a certain element of curiosity with respect to their environment....In our continuing efforts to a better and better understanding of things which perhaps we shall not fully understand for many centuries yet to come, if ever, we find the greatest interest and the most driving motive in the pursuit of scientific studies.[46]

45. Harvey B. Lemon, "New Vistas of Atomic Structure," *The Scientific Monthly* 17 (1923): 181.

46. Harvey B. Lemon and Niel F. Beardsley, *Experimental Mechanics: An Analytical College Text* (Chicago, 1935), 6.

THE HUMANITIES AND SOCIAL SCIENCES GENERAL COURSES

I f the two natural-sciences courses emerged from curricular projects of the 1920s, the new general Humanities course had an even deeper institutional history. The main architect was an elderly history professor, Ferdinand Schevill, whose initial appointment to Chicago originated in 1892. Schevill had a fascinating career. Born in Cincinnati in 1868 Schevill attended Yale University as an undergraduate, at the same time that William Rainey Harper was on the faculty. Schevill took Harper's course on the Hebrew prophets, establishing a personal relationship that eventually led to Schevill's coming to Chicago. After graduating from Yale he went to Germany to study for a PhD in history, working at the University of Freiburg with, among others, Hermann von Holst. In 1892 Harper offered Schevill a job for eight hundred dollars as an "Assistant in History" on the recommendation of Charles F. Kent, a former student of Harper's at Yale who was studying Hebrew in Berlin and who reminded Harper that Schevill was one of the "brightest men" in the Yale graduating class of 1889.[47] Such informality was typical of the times,

47. Kent to Harper, October 1, 1891, William Rainey Harper Papers, box 14, folder 30. Schevill's birth name was Schwill, which he anglicized in 1909. Urged by Kent, Schevill wrote to Harper on October 17, 1891, re-introducing himself and presenting his credentials. Schevill to Harper, October 17, 1891, ibid. Harper received a similar suggestion from George S. Goodspeed, who informed Harper of a recent meeting with Schevill and who allowed that "he…strikes me as a very bright man. I think if you could put him in as a docent at Chicago, you would not be mistaken at all." Goodspeed to Harper, October 25, 1891, ibid., box 12, folder 34.

and Schevill came to Chicago knowing little or nothing of the prehistory of the new University.

Ferdinand Schevill soon proved to be an amiable colleague and a brilliant teacher.[48] He was particularly close to a remarkable social circle of young humanists in the later 1890s who met regularly and included John Mathews Manly, Robert Herrick, Robert Lovett, and William Vaughn Moody, a reminder of how dependent the early faculty were on each other for intellectual and cultural sustenance.[49] Schevill never liked the University as an administrative community, and when he warned his personal friend Frank Lloyd Wright that the University High School was like "all schools, established churches, minister-blest marriages, and all other sacred institutions" in that "to play with any one of them is alas! alas! to toss yourself into a buzz-saw," he was alluding to his own iconoclastic relationship with Chicago.[50]

48. The distinguished American historian Howard K. Beale of the University of Wisconsin many years later remembered that Schevill "was the greatest teacher I had ever sat under. He was, of course, one of the most cultivated persons and delightful companions I have ever known. Above all else he was a great human being. I still feel the inspiration he gave me when I took his courses as an undergraduate." Beale to James L. Cate, December 31, 1956, James L. Cate Papers, box 4.

49. Robert M. Lovett, *All Our Years: The Autobiography of Robert Morss Lovett* (New York, 1948), 97–98. Robert Herrick later remembered: "The half dozen of us young men who had come to the new world together naturally formed the closest sort of fellowship. We were like a company of the celebrated musketeers, disturbers of the academic peace and scoffers often, but really devoted to our work and faithful. We may have cast regretful glances half of homesickness backward to that pleasant East from which we came, but we were faithful to the hope of the West." "Going West," 6–7, Robert Herrick Papers, box 3, folder 10.

50. Schevill to Wright, September 4, 1916, Frank Lloyd Wright Papers, microfiche copy at the Getty Research Institute.

Schevill began his scholarly career with studies of the medieval Italian communes. His first major book was a study of the free republic of Siena in the thirteenth and fourteenth centuries, and it highlighted a major theme in Schevill's thought: the tension between the universal and the particular, between monarchy, which represented order and civility, and communal self-government, which sponsored freedom and democracy. Schevill believed that free communes like Siena had "endowed man with a new conception of his powers and purposes." They created "a new civilization, a civilization, in fact, with the elaboration of which the world had been occupied down to our own day."[51] A similar conceptual framework informed Schevill's later book on the Renaissance city-state of Florence, published in 1936. Schevill would later argue that both of these impulses—order and freedom—were already present in the ancient world, and that it was thus logical to begin the study of European civilization with Greece and Rome.[52] Of the many members of the early Chicago faculty who had studied in Europe, Ferdinand Schevill was perhaps the one most transformed by European values and European culture. He once confessed to his friend Sherwood Anderson, "in America I often have the feeling that I belong to Europe, and in Europe I reach the deep

51. Ferdinand Schevill, *Siena, the Story of a Medieval Commune* (New York, 1909), 420–21.

52. "The outstanding forms evolved by the Mediterranean peoples are two: monarchy and the self-governing city-state. Monarchy represents the tendency toward unity and peace; the city-state the tendency towards freedom and self-determination. The balance between unity and freedom is indicated as the political problem of mankind." Schevill to Baker Brownell, November 26, 1924, Baker Brownell Papers, box 9, folder 4, Northwestern University Archives. See also Ferdinand Schevill, "Man's Political History," in *Man and His World: Northwestern University Essays in Contemporary Thought*, ed. Baker Brownell, vol. 4, *Making Mankind* (New York, 1929), 145–76.

conclusion that my roots are in American soil."[53] He traveled frequently across Europe, gaining an intimate, firsthand knowledge of European art and architecture and often took friends and the children of colleagues on cycling and walking tours of France, Germany, and his beloved Italy.[54]

During World War I Schevill was one of a small minority of faculty who opposed America's entrance into the war, further isolating him from the mainline faculty politics of Chicago, and by the early 1920s he had tired of teaching, indicating to President Ernest D. Burton in 1923 that he intended to resign to pursue a full-time career in writing.[55] Burton persuaded Schevill to stay on a part-time basis until 1927, when he left the University for good, or so he thought. Schevill had looked forward to a life beyond the institutional claims of the University, but by 1930 he was almost broke, having loaned substantial sums to friends who were in distress because of the Depression, and part of his motivation to return to teaching may have been financial urgency.[56] When Boucher contacted him in early 1931 about returning to the University to take up the great challenge of the new Humanities course, Schevill was thus easily persuaded both by the substantial salary that Boucher offered him and by

53. Schevill to Sherwood Anderson, written while Schevill was visiting Vienna, November 13, 1927, Sherwood Anderson Papers, box 27, Newberry Library.

54. See, for example, Lovett, *All Our Years*, 71-89, 106–20; William Vaughn Moody, "European Diary," 28–33, William Vaughn Moody Papers, box 1, folder 9. The Chicago sociologist Everett C. Hughes later remembered that Schevill took the son of W. I. Thomas on a walking tour of Italy. Hughes to Mary Bolton Wirth, May 31, 1968, Mary Bolton Wirth Papers, box 5, folder 1.

55. Schevill to Burton, December 27, 1923, Presidents' Papers, 1889–1925, box 59, folder 21.

56. Schevill to Frank Lloyd Wright, October 19, 1930, Frank Lloyd Wright Papers. Schevill also faced heavy medical bills arising from his wife's illness.

the challenge to finally leave his mark on the teaching of European civilization to newly minted college students.[57]

World War I had come as a deep shock to Ferdinand Schevill, who believed that the war had threatened the fundamental values of cultural balance and material progress that had marked European civilization up to 1914. The world of the 1920s was one dominated by "revolutionary monstrosities" in Europe and "heaped-up wealth" in America.[58] For a bourgeois humanist rooted in the culture of late nineteenth-century Central Europe, both continents seemed to be veering off course, into crass materialism and social upheaval. To Frank Lloyd Wright Schevill argued in 1927, "ours is a government by the mob," and by 1932 he would insist that

> the more I turn the present difficulties over in my mind, the more convinced I am the issue is quite simply between two kinds of society. Either the acquisitive society we've got or a friendly commonwealth of approximate economic equals. Maybe the acquisitive society is all we are capable of with our inheritance and animal equipment. In that case we shall continue to struggle in the back slough in which the human race has been immersed from the beginning. But if we are to make a try for the other thing—and I say, let's go—we ought to be perfectly clear that it is a whole-

57. Boucher to Filbey and Woodward, March 13, 1931, Dean of the College Records, 1923–1958, box 7, folder 2. Schevill was offered an annual salary of $7,500, a very substantial sum for the time.

58. Schevill to Anderson, September 22, 1923, and November 13, 1927, Sherwood Anderson Papers, box 27.

hog or nothing proposition and that pacifism, third-parties and melioratives are distractions that darken the issue.[59]

Schevill was a prolific writer, espousing the nineteenth-century European tradition of writing history for the educated general reader. He once argued that

> I kept in mind a prospective audience, composed, not of a small group of specialists, but of that larger body of men and women who constitute a spiritual brotherhood by reason of their common interest in the treasure of the past....I make bold to affirm my belief that scholarship practiced as the secret cult of a few initiates, amidst the jealous and watchful exclusion of the public, may indeed succeed in preserving its principles from contamination, but must pay for the immunity obtained with the failure of the social and educational purposes which are its noblest justification.[60]

Schevill thus believed that history's largest purpose was to ennoble as well as to educate the general reader, and in his teaching at the University of Chicago he pursued the same objectives, making him an ideal and much cherished teacher who sought to encourage the student's cultural self-development and intellectual maturity. In a sense, Schevill was deeply involved in the project of general education long before the phrase became a popular educational concept in the 1930s and 1940s.

59. Schevill to Wright, February 16, 1927, Frank Lloyd Wright Papers; Schevill to Anderson, September 26, 1932, Sherwood Anderson Papers, box 27.

60. Schevill, *Siena*, v.

Schevill's most successful book was his *History of Modern Europe*, first published in 1898 and revised continuously until 1946. The 1925 edition reveals many of the arguments that would have informed his approach to teaching European history. Schevill believed that Europe had over a thousand years nurtured a European civilization that was perhaps the most powerful and far-reaching of world civilizations, since it included the United States within its cultural and intellectual compass. The United States was a "passionate, struggling, and inseparable element" of a larger European civilization, and this gave special urgency and authority to the project of teaching European history to young Americans.[61] Yet after World War I, a war that he profoundly regretted, Ferdinand Schevill's story of a slow, but positive evolution of European civilization was vastly complicated by the ruptures of the Treaty of Versailles. By the later 1920s, he was in the fascinating but also perplexing situation of having to imagine the portrait of a Europe that he viewed with both admiration and disillusionment, which could be proffered to young Americans. In the end, the course that he designed was much more of the first than the second, having little to do with a twentieth century that Schevill found dispiriting and depressing.

Schevill was assisted by Arthur P. Scott, then a mid-career associate professor of history who was a departmental jack-of-all-trades, and (to a much lesser extent) by Hayward Keniston, an associate professor of Spanish philology and comparative linguistics who eventually left Chicago for the University of Michigan. A graduate of Princeton, Scott had received his PhD from Chicago in 1916. Scott had lived for several years in Beirut and had a special interest in the expansion of Europe. He was also an authority on colonial American law, publishing a book on criminal law

61. Ferdinand Schevill, *A History of Europe from the Reformation to Our Own Day* (New York, 1925), 4.

in colonial Virginia, and he regularly taught courses on US history as well. In the 1920s he taught an introductory survey in the Department of History on the History of European Civilization, based on a strict chronological framework. The new Humanities general-education survey was a collaborative effort, but Ferdinand Schevill provided the major intellectual imprint on its formation.[62] Arthur Scott later recalled: "we used to say that whatever the course did for the students, it certainly educated the staff; and no small element in our education was the intimate and informal contacts with the leader whom we usually addressed as Maestro, and referred to as the Old Master."[63] When Schevill died in 1954, Norman Maclean remembered of the founding of the course in 1931: "in the history of our university, this moment itself was a Renaissance and the atmosphere was charged with excitement, defiance, and promise of adventure." For Maclean, Schevill's humanism lay at the heart of the course, a humanism that was itself "a form of art. He was a historian of man's creative activity, and so the Renaissance was his home and Florence was his city. By this, I mean something more than that he loved architecture, painting, sculpture, literature, and music. I mean that he viewed man's other activities—economic and political and social—as themselves manifestations of the creative spirit which when fully flourishing as in Florence, is dominated by a desire to attain beauty."[64]

62. See Schevill to Boucher, April 23, 1931, Dean of the College Records, 1923–1958, box 7, folder 2.

63. Arthur Scott, eulogy for Ferdinand Schevill, 1955, Cate Papers, box 4; and C. Phillip Miller to James L. Cate, March 9, 1955, ibid.

64. Norman Maclean, eulogy for Ferdinand Schevill, 1955, ibid.

Schevill, Scott, and Keniston fashioned a course that wove together strands of other courses they had taught in the 1910s and 1920s.[65] The purpose of the course was to expose students to "the cultural history of mankind as a continuum and as a whole."[66] Although colleagues in the Social Sciences later tagged the course as being primarily "aesthetic" and neglecting political and social history, this was not quite true. Framing lectures did provide key chronology, but much of the course was on the history of European ideas, as represented by significant writers and thinkers. Students were expected to read substantial parts of classics like (among many others) the *Iliad* and *Odyssey*, Herodotus, Thucydides, the Bible, Dante, Chaucer, Molière, Luther, Shakespeare, Voltaire, Rousseau, Goethe, Darwin, and Walt Whitman. Many individual poems and other shorter pieces were also assigned. The aim of the course was to use "history as a foundation and framework for the presentation of the religion, philosophy, literature and art of the civilizations which have contributed most conspicuously to the shaping of the contemporary outlook on life," beginning with the civilizations of the Nile and the Tigris-Euphrates valleys, Greece and Rome, and concluding with "our ruling western civilization," the latter being "the main object of attention."[67] Intellectually, it was clearly the most conservative of the four new general courses, since

65. It might be argued that Boucher privileged his own department in giving the historians the primary charge of organizing the Humanities general course. The department had adopted a resolution in early 1931 urging Boucher "to retain the course on the History of Civilization as part of the offering of either the Humanities or the Social Sciences Division or both." Boucher's decision to appoint Schevill did essentially that. "Minutes of the Department of History, January 24, 1931," Department of History Records, box 19, folder 4.

66. "Preliminary Report of the Committee in Charge of the General Courses in the Humanities," Dean of the College Records, 1923–1958, box 7, folder 2.

67. Schevill, "Humanities," [April 1931], ibid.

it did not seek to break new ground in pedagogical methods or in scholarly design. The logic of the course was to convey the rich tapestry of the
European tradition, but a tradition that had experienced profound rup-
ture between 1914 and 1918. The course dealt with World War I and its
aftermath in only two lectures, perhaps because Schevill himself was so
disillusioned by it.[68]

Although the history of Western civilization from the ancient world
to contemporary times became the organizing axis, much attention was
also paid to European literature, art, and architecture. American literature
was also included, both for a sense of time and place, but also in a bow to
Schevill's notion that America was also a part of Western civilization.
The works of art examined in the course were treated in a strongly con-
textualist mode, or as a later commentary noted "that ideas and works
of art are related to the *life* out of which they arise"[69] The course was an
obvious target for formalists who cared little or nothing about the
encrusted historical exemplariness of their texts and more about the
intrinsic structural properties that defined them as works of art. Still,
the course styled itself as closely attentive to the development of analytic
skills and aesthetic judgment. As Arthur Scott put it in 1933, the
Humanities course aimed to convey a certain amount of information

68. In fact, the initial outline proposed in April 1931, had nothing on the twentieth century, aside from a final lecture on "This Plural World: The Reigning
Confusion in Our Intellectual and Aesthetic Outlook." The first syllabus published in September 1931 commented that "the modern world of science and
machines, of national states and world empires, has set in motion forces which
seem to have got out of hand and threaten, like Frankenstein's monster, to
destroy the civilization which gave rise to them." *Introductory General Course in
the Humanities Syllabus* (Chicago, 1931), 328.

69. Arthur P. Scott, "The Humanities General Course. Statement of Objectives,"
May 1939, Dean of the College Records, 1923–1958, box 6, folder 9.

about European culture that would be of "practical value to young
people presently to be adult members of twentieth century American
society." But it also sought, "to the limits of its collective ingenuity," to
encourage and to give practice to "straight and independent habits of
thinking, as by-products of which it may fondly be hoped that a more
critical, rational, tolerant, and broad-minded attitude may be fostered."[70]

To operationalize the course Schevill needed young assistants, and
he found three dedicated men in Norman F. Maclean, Eugene N. Ander-
son, and James L. Cate. Cate, a young medievalist from Texas, and
Anderson, a young German historian from Nebraska, had studied with
Schevill and Scott and were hired first. Cate in turn told Schevill and
Scott about Norman Maclean and persuaded them to hire his fellow
Westerner from Montana who was a graduate student in the Department
of English. The chance to join what he viewed at the time as a truly revolutionary teaching project was a decisive moment for Maclean. Chauncey
Boucher later described Maclean's work in the Humanities general
course as the product of a "choice soul and a teaching genius....His hold
upon students is most remarkable."[71] Many years later Maclean wrote to
Frances Cate, Jimmie Cate's widow, remembering that Schevill and Scott
had looked for "young men who like them were warm-hearted, humor-
ous, and wide-ranging in their interests" and that the chance to teach
in the new Humanities course between 1931 and 1937 had offered "the
happiest and most exciting years of our lives."[72]

70. Scott to Boucher, November 1, 1933, Dean of the College Records, 1923–
1958, box 7, folder 2.

71. Boucher's evaluation, dated 1935, is in the Presidents' Papers, 1925–1940,
box 42, folder 1.

72. "Remember...all the excitement of those days of the new Hutchins College,
and the wonderful warm times we had when our staff was invited to Books-

The course consisted of ninety lectures of fifty minutes each over three quarters, with one discussion session a week for twenty-five students that focused on an intensive discussion of an assigned original document or documents. Schevill and Scott gave most of the lectures, but they also recruited other luminaries from the Humanities, like Paul Shorey, T. V. Smith, James W. Thompson, William Craigie, Shailer Mathews, and Robert Lovett, to offer single lectures on subjects close to their research competency. The lectures were organized linearly along a chronological trajectory and combined narrative social and political history with studies of novels and works of art. At first several fragments of texts were discussed each week, but by the mid-1930s, the course had settled into a pattern of assigning one notable work—a novel, a poem, or a piece of nonfiction—each week for discussion, thirty in all through the academic year. The lectures did not duplicate the reading assignments, but were meant as introductions to broad debates or as portraits of a Weltanschauung of a historical era. The course was replete with facts and dates, but also had a more ambitious agenda in that it hoped to encourage analytic study skills and intellectual self-confidence among its students.[73] Much of this happened outside of class, in small groups run by Cate, Maclean, and others. William H. McNeill, who was a student

wallow." Maclean to Frances Cate, November 6, 1981, Norman Maclean Papers, box 15.

73. Maclean remembered about James Cate's discussion groups: "Jimmie really ran discussion groups. They were really 'question hours'. Jimmie pursued his students with shrewd, unrelenting questions until he caught them with the answer, and 'I don't know' was never an answer to him. To him, you always knew the answer, if you only knew how to find it. And I feel that his greatest professional joy was in teaching and seeing his students's discovering with joy that they really knew the answer." Ibid.

in Maclean's discussion group of the Humanities course in 1934–35, later recalled the scene in Maclean's office where

> you [Maclean] used to assemble a group of eager beavers to talk about anything and everything. The kernel of this group later migrated to the Beta house and became the protagonists of the marathon bull sessions on whose margins I wafted through college. You, of course, were the catalyst, and thereby created the micro-environment of my college days, an environment which still seems so marvelous to me that I cannot really believe that others since have ever attained such heights as we, foolish and sophomoric as we must have been, then scaled.[74]

The Humanities course was in some respects as self-consciously skills oriented as was its latter-day heir, the History of Western Civilization course of the 1950s, but it did insist that European civilization itself bore within it the fate of modern man, and that in studying this fate, American university students would come to appreciate and analyze their own situations more acutely and self-consciously.

The year-long Social Sciences course for first-year students, Social Sciences I, was organized by three young professors, Harry Gideonse, Jerome Kerwin, and Louis Wirth. Each of these men represented a different discipline, each was to become an authority in his field, and each had clear personal connections to the "real" world of social-science praxis that began to define the conduct of general education in the 1930s.[75] An

74. McNeill to Maclean, January 29, 1966, Maclean Papers, box 18.

75. "Perhaps the most important result of the association of the graduate and professional schools with the college is the influence of research upon the general educational process.... There is an increasing disposition on the part of students

economist, Harry D. Gideonse served as the chair of the course and was its most articulate spokesman.[76] Born in the Netherlands and trained in chemistry and economics at Columbia University and the University of Geneva, Gideonse wrote his doctoral dissertation on the war debts generated by World War I. He worked for an international student organization in Geneva for several years, was fluent in French and German, and had strong credentials in international relations and international trade. Gideonse was hired by the Department of Economics from Rutgers University as an untenured associate professor in 1930, with the expectation that he would be tenured within three years.[77] Gideonse was an acerbic, scrappy person, with an outgoing personality and quick wit who sometimes came across as overly cocky and even vain.[78] He was a very effective public intellectual and participated regularly for seven years in the University's Round Table radio program, speaking out on

to seek the classrooms of teachers who are known by their criticism of society to be realistic and fearless....Research will replace tradition and authority in determining the beliefs by which men live." See Robert M. Lovett, "The Cleavage between College and Life," 6–7, Robert M. Lovett Papers, box 2, folder 17.

76. Boucher first appointed Gideonse to lead the course, who then recruited Wirth and Kerwin to join him. See "The General Course for Freshmen in the Social Sciences, April, 1931," Dean of the College Records, 1923–1958, box 15, folder 3. Gideonse, Wirth, and Kerwin also organized a second year-long course in the Social Sciences for students wishing to major in one of the Social Science disciplines, but since this course was not required of all New Plan students, my discussion in the present essay will focus on the Introductory Course.

77. "If at the end of the period indicated [i.e., 1933] the relationship was mutually satisfactory, we should expect your tenure to become indeterminate." H. A. Millis to Gideonse, February 6, 1930, Presidents' Papers, Appointments and Budgets, box 25, folder 5.

78. "Gideonse is very able and nice, but something of a 'blowhard'." William T. Hutchinson Diary, entry of January 19, 1936.

public-policy issues relating to domestic and international affairs. Charles Merriam characterized Gideonse as an excellent lecturer, but also as an "indoctrinator," and Merriam did not mean this in a wholly flattering way.[79] As we will see below, Gideonse soon found himself on a collision course with Robert Hutchins over the meaning of general education, since he violently opposed Hutchins's attempts to impose what Gideonse felt to be a backward-oriented, great-books program at Chicago. In 1938 Gideonse was offered a tenured full professorship at Barnard College, which Hutchins refused to match, thereby forcing Gideonse out of the University. Gideonse soon left Barnard to become the second president of Brooklyn College, where he served with distinction until 1966 but amid some controversy over his staunch opposition to left-wing radicalism in the New York City unions.

Jerome G. Kerwin received his PhD in political philosophy at Columbia University in 1926. In 1923 Charles Merriam recruited him to join the faculty of the Department of Political Science at Chicago as an instructor. Kerwin quickly became a protégé of Merriam, with Merriam personally introducing him to the vagaries of Chicago municipal politics. Kerwin immediately became engaged in local reform activities, like investigating illegal polling practices in Hinky-Dinky Kenna's First Ward during the 1924 mayoral elections in Chicago. Throughout his career Kerwin encouraged his students to become involved in local politics, and he took pride that his former students as diverse as Leon Despres, Charles Percy, and Robert Merriam had followed his lead. Kerwin devoted much of his career to exploring the complex issues of church and state in American political culture, but he also wrote important books on schools and city government, on federal water-power

79. "Minutes of the Sub-Committee on Curriculum, February 4, 1935," 6, Division of the Social Sciences Records, box 16.

legislation, on civil-military relationships in American life, and on the idea of democracy. A devout Catholic, Kerwin helped to found the local Roman Catholic Calvert House in 1953. Kerwin immediately proved himself an immensely popular undergraduate teacher (when he considered leaving Chicago for Dartmouth in 1928, six hundred students signed a petition urging him to stay), so it was hardly surprising that Boucher recruited him to the team charged with organizing the new course. Of his collaboration with Gideonse and Wirth, Kerwin later recalled, "as we were from three different disciplines, it took three or four months for us to understand each other." Given the enormous intellectual range that the new Social Sciences course sought to cover, Kerwin found the new course to be "the hardest job of teaching I ever attempted."[80]

Louis Wirth was the most distinguished scholar of the group. Born to a Jewish farming family in Gmünden, a small Rhenish town in Germany, Wirth was sent in 1911 to live with an uncle in Omaha, Nebraska. He decided to remain in America, attended the College of the University of Chicago between 1916 and 1919, and stayed on to take his PhD in sociology. His teachers in graduate school were the great sociologists Albion Small, Robert Park, Ellsworth Faris, and William Burgess, but as an undergraduate, Wirth studied history as well as sociology and had eight courses in modern European history and modern American history. Wirth was one of a small group of campus leftists during World War I, and his presence was widely known, so much so that he ran afoul of the University administration in 1919. Wirth was a leader of the Cosmopolitan Club, a group of international students. He was also a student radical who opposed American intervention in World War I. In

80. *Chicago Maroon*, November 18, 1960, 20.

the weeks before graduation in June 1919, Wirth gave a speech at a meeting of the Cosmopolitan Club denouncing the Treaty of Versailles as "the most impudent document ever devised by the hands and brains of diplomats."[81] Fred Merrifield, an assistant professor of New Testament studies and the faculty advisor to the Cosmopolitan Club, reported to President Harry Pratt Judson on Wirth's sentiments, accusing him of being a "clever orator, cool, and daring" who opposed all established governments and of being "in favor of revolution."[82] Judson thereupon took the astonishing step of summoning an emergency meeting of the full professors of the arts and sciences to consider whether to withhold granting Wirth and Ephraim Gottlieb, another student radical, their

81. *Chicago Tribune*, June 7, 1919, 3.

82. See the memorandum in the Presidents' Papers, 1889–1925, box 69, folder 3; and the unsigned statement, written after May 14, 1919, in the Ernest Burgess Papers, box 6, folder 11, reporting: "there was in existence among certain member[s] of the Club of a disposition to conduct the affairs of the Club House in accordance with Bolschevistic or anarchistic principles. This manifested itself in expressions of opposition to University regulation, and in declarations of intentions to observe only those which were approved by the individuals." Fred Merrifield then had a direct collision with Louis Wirth at a meeting of the Cosmopolitan Club three days after Judson had attempted to have him expelled. Merrifield reported to Judson that Wirth had accused him of insulting students who were Jewish, that Wirth "cast slurs on my divinity (religious) work, insinuating that this work was carried on insincerely" and also that Wirth "drew out a petition, signed by numerous members, some signature taken in my presence with most insulting looks cast my way, to throw me out of the club." Fred Merrifield, "Insulting Remarks Addressed to Faculty Members at the Recent Cosmopolitan Meeting, Sunday, June 8th [1919]," Presidents' Papers, 1889–1925, box 31, folder 8. Merrifield was himself a graduate of the university and the Divinity School. He had spent several years in Japan and had the claim to fame of having introduced baseball to the Japanese. As a scholar, he was not particularly distinguished.

BA degrees, which would have been legally tantamount to expulsion.[83] Clearly, Judson wanted Wirth to be evicted, but Ferdinand Schevill and Albion Small made a point of attending the meeting and spoke out strongly in Wirth's defense.[84] As a college student Wirth had had three history courses with Schevill, including Schevill's two-quarter graduate course on the History of Civilization, for which Wirth merited As.[85] As profoundly different as these two men were—the one a young German Jew who had become a left-wing radical during his three years on campus and who was accused by Merrifield of being a Bolshevik, the other a

83. "Minutes of the Faculty of the Arts, Literature, and Science, Special Meeting, June 5, 1919," 1; *Chicago Tribune*, June 7, 1919, 3.

84. See the later memoir of Mary Bolton Wirth, "1916–1920 at the University of Chicago," 2. Mary Wirth, who was also an undergraduate at Chicago during the war, described in graphic detail the stolid campus political atmosphere presided over by President Harry Pratt Judson. She insisted that Ferdinand Schevill and his wife used their home to provide bond money for a local radical student arrested in late 1919 and early 1920 in the so-called "post-Palmer raids": "Professor and Mrs. Schevill put up their home as bond and the case was continued for nearly eight years during which time this student—considered the most 'dangerous' of our days—had become a successful and conservative businessman in the State of Missouri. The Schevills were in a position for years where they could not sell their house because of the bond." Ibid., 3-4. Schevill sold the house to Everett C. Hughes in 1944, who later recalled that Schevill stopped by several times just to see the place again. Hughes to Mary Wirth, May 31, 1968. Both documents are in the Mary Bolton Wirth Papers, box 1, folder 1 and 2.

85. Schevill himself considered that this course was a prototype of the history he intended to write in the mid- and later 1920s. In his letter of resignation to Ernest D. Burton Schevill observed: "my courses in the History of Civilization may give you a general idea of the kind of thing which has taken possession of me and which I wish to bring to some sort of conclusion before the Referee calls Time and it is too late." Schevill to Burton, December 27, 1923, Presidents' Papers, 1889–1925, box 59, folder 21.

middle-aged German American whose life and career had made him into a kind of late nineteenth-century German *Bildungsbürger* deeply in love with Italian culture but fated to live his life in the American Midwest—both were opposed to the war, and both were shocked by the social inequalities it summoned forth and by its flawed diplomatic resolution in 1919.[86] The assembled faculty had the good sense to reject Judson's ploy. As Robert Lovett, another disillusioned senior faculty member who had lost a son in the war, later recalled, the "two students, about to graduate, made caustic criticisms of the Treaty of Versailles at a dinner of the International Club, which were reported by faculty spies. The president summoned the faculty to consider the question of withholding their degrees, and was unanimously told that if approval of the Treaty was to be required for a degree, it should be so stated in the entrance requirements."[87]

By the early 1930s Wirth was on his way to become one of the most important urban sociologists of his generation, but his notions about how to teach social science to beginning undergraduates were profoundly affected by his personal interest in large cities like Chicago.[88] Having

86. Schevill's deep unhappiness with the Treaty of Versailles is clear in the 1925 edition of his *A History of Europe*: "The new boundaries were drawn by a group of victors with the conscious purpose of doing the vanquished as much injury as possible" (696).

87. Robert M. Lovett, "Democracy in Colleges," 6, unpublished and undated manuscript, Robert Lovett Papers, box 2, folder 17.

88. "Mary and Louis Wirth were young radicals and social workers together; Louis spent a day or two in jail at the time of the Palmer raids (1920?)." Everett Hughes to Winifred Raudenbush, June 24, 1966, Robert Park Papers, box 19, folder 6. For Wirth as a teacher see Edward Shils, *A Fragment of a Sociological Autobiography: The History of My Pursuit of a Few Ideas* (New Brunswick, NJ, 2006), 44–46. I owe this reference to Terry N. Clark.

Louis Wirth, photo by LIFE *magazine, 1945*

worked for the Jewish Charities of Chicago, helping immigrant families in the early 1920s, Wirth had a deep interest in translating social theory into social action. After rejoining the faculty as an assistant professor in 1931, he became involved in a myriad of municipal reform activities, serving as president of the American Council on Race Relations, as the director of planning for the Illinois Planning Commission, and as an advisor to many local community and business groups in Chicago. He was courageous enough to call for an end to the terrible real estate covenants that blocked African Americans in Chicago from moving into Hyde Park and Woodlawn.

One of the main intellectual goals of the new Social Sciences course was to help students understand the complexities of urban industrial civilization, and it could do this so effectively because its students lived and worked in the vast social laboratory that Chicago represented. Given the strong interest of Jerome Kerwin and Louis Wirth in using Chicago as a social laboratory for their teaching, it was not surprising that the course even arranged for students to visit the Stock Exchange, the Board of Trade, Armour and Company, and the International Harvester Company, as well as unemployment offices, slums, and housing projects.[89] In addition to these formal visits, which were carefully planned to illustrate lecture or discussion topics in the course, the organizers also staged smaller events away from campus, including a group of fifty students at Druce Lake, who heard the young Reinhold Niebuhr discuss the (in his view) deeply flawed nature of American capitalism. Not surprisingly, Harry Gideonse sharply opposed this view, and the students found themselves in a two-day donnybrook that left them better informed about both positions. Another group of students organized a three-day retreat on international relations at Lakeside, Michigan, which discussed (among other topics) whether the United States should belatedly join the League of Nations. One of the Social Sciences course's discussion leaders, Mary Gilson, observed of the latter event: "At this conference as well as the Druce Lake Conference the New Plan students stood head and shoulders above the others. This was so noticeable in relation to both their grasp of the subjects discussed and their phrasing of questions that one of the old plan students said to me 'We old plan students are at a disadvantage at these conferences for you can see what a difference the

89. Gilson to Boucher, May 11, 1933, Dean of the College Records, 1923–1958, box 8, folder 2.

New Plan training has made when you hear the freshmen and sopho-
mores in discussion'."[90] Such visits and symposia also helped to modulate
the heavy emphasis on text-based readings, and as Walter Laves later
observed, "this promises to become one of the richest aspects of the
course to the students and is really only possible on a systematic basis
when the staff and student body are sufficiently large—as in our present
College course—to warrant a thoroughgoing effort."[91]

The Social Sciences course did not attempt to give a panoramic overview of the social sciences, since Gideonse, Kerwin, and Wirth felt that
this was conceptually impossible. Rather the course focused on three
large problems and approached them with the theoretical apparatus of
three different disciplines, which they believed would be vastly superior
to existing introductory courses, which "must everywhere, for obvious
reasons, be superficial and unsatisfactory."[92] The main theme of the new
course was the "impact of the complex of forces that is generally described
as the industrial revolution on economic, social, and political institutions."[93] The first quarter, taught by Gideonse, stressed the role of industrial change in England and in contemporary America, where students
were asked to read R. H. Tawney, *The Acquisitive Society*, Lewis Mum-
ford, *The Story of Utopias*, Herbert Hoover, *American Individualism*,

90. Gilson to Boucher, May 11, 1933, ibid.

91. Walter H. Laves, "Report on the First Year of the Introductory Course in
the Social Sciences," 12–13, Dean of the College Records, 1923–1958, box 8,
folder 2.

92. See Gideonse, Wirth, and Kerwin to the Social Sciences Faculty, May 15,
1931, 1, ibid.

93. "The General Course (for Freshmen) in the Social Sciences," April, 1931,
ibid.

and Norman Thomas, *America's Way Out*, in order to explore the development and general characteristics of the present economic order. The second quarter, taught by Wirth, took up questions of the impact of scientific and technological progress on modern society, studying population movements from rural to urban areas, the ways in which the new industrial-technological order had accelerated large-scale social change, the growth of large cities, and the emergence of new kinds of "culture" in place of societies with strong notions of customary traditions. This quarter used books such as W. G. Sumner's *Folkways*, Franz Boas's *The Mind of Primitive Man*, and the classic work by Robert and Helen Lynd, *Middletown: A Study in Contemporary American Culture*. The final quarter, taught by Kerwin, focused on the modern state—and especially central government—as a premier locus of political and economic control, with students exploring the growth of governmental authority and bureaucratic control in the industrial world.[94] In this quarter students read Charles A. Beard, *American Government and Politics*, Harold Laski, *Politics*, Graham Wallas, *Human Nature in Politics*, and Gilbert Murray, *The Ordeal of This Generation*. The course ended with six lectures offered by Gideonse that tied the various themes together. In addition to these books, students also read essays by (among others) Adam Smith, Karl Marx, Immanuel Kant, T. R. Malthus, Thomas Paine, Ruth Benedict, Charles Beard, Charles H. Cooley, Robert E. Park, William F. Ogburn, Edward Sapir, and John Dewey—a veritable who's who of modern social and political thought.

Seen three-quarters of a century later, the Social Sciences general course looks like an enterprise invented in the midst of the vast displacements of the Great Depression, with both teachers and students alike

94. See Gideonse's testimony about the course during the Walgreen investigation, May 24, 1935, Laird Bell Papers, box 8, folder 8.

confronting the collapse or near collapse of liberal societies in Europe and America. Ostensibly about the origins and development of industrial society, the course raised profound issues about the fate of individualism and personal freedom in the face of the challenges that communism and fascism presented to European liberalism and American democracy. In seeking to analyze how the West became enveloped in the industrial world of the nineteenth century, the course also weighed America and Europe's common but perilous future in the twentieth century, concluding with lectures on the rise of international cooperation and the options for the future determination of peace. The course's very lack of a single overarching theme or interpretative standpoint was quite deliberate. Intellectual pluralism, within a schema broadly sympathetic to industrial capitalism, would contrast with the mistaken hopes of utopians, whether on the left or the right. In an inadvertent claim that revealed much about the course, Gideonse would later insist, "a course that pulled *everything* together quite systematically would not be true to life, and could only exist on the basis of some totalitarian philosophy of the Marxist, Thomist, or Fascist type.[95] The reference to Thomism as a "totalitarian philosophy" was for local consumption in Hyde Park, and we will return to this invocation shortly.

The Social Sciences course prided itself on having lectures that were not repetitions of material from the syllabus, which resulted in more students attending than might otherwise have been the case and thereby encouraged "the greatest stimulation of original thinking and interest." In contrast to the other courses that relied on visiting instructors who were often men of great prestige, the Social Sciences course had the advantage of allowing the students to get to know the ideas and

95. Gideonse to Brumbaugh, October 31, 1935, 4, Dean of the College Records, 1923–1958, box 8, folder 2.

personality of one person for a "long period of systematic attention."[96] Although discussion sections were voluntary, as late as 1940 Walter Laves estimated that at least two-thirds of the 750 students enrolled in the course faithfully participated in these exercises for all three quarters.

The published syllabi were equally noteworthy, since they provided all students with a "common field of reference" that they might rely upon to understand the lectures and other assigned readings, and thus helped to create intellectual anchors for the course. Given that the previous academic preparation that individual students brought to the general-education courses was extremely varied, the common syllabi and common readings created an even playing field for all students to perform as effectively as possible.

OPERATIONALIZING THE NEW CURRICULUM

 nce the planning groups had developed the plans for their courses, Dean of the College Chauncey Boucher sent their proposed syllabi to other, more senior members of various departments for their comments. Given the coalition nature of the courses in the biological and physical sciences, most colleagues either accepted the outlines, or were indifferent to the projects, once it was clear that students seeking advanced training in the natural sciences could also select more specialized science sequences as free electives to supplement the work of the general surveys.[97] Among

96. Walter H. Laves, "Report on the First Year of the Introductory Course in the Social Sciences," 3.

97. Mortimer Adler was Hutchins's mole on the deliberations of the first curriculum committee in 1930–31 and reported on the strident demands of

the humanists, the New Plan encountered skepticism from John Mat-
thews Manly, the chair of the Department of English, who thought that
the system of comprehensive examinations would be difficult to sustain
and also worried that students would lack proper assistance "in determining their field of specialization early in their college course." The
Humanities course itself earned a rebuke from Shailer Mathews, who
complained about the absence of religion in the syllabus. But in general,
faculty opinion deferred to Boucher and especially to Schevill, who had
great prestige in the division.[98] The Social Sciences course became, in
contrast, the object of considerable acrimony from the start, meeting
with heated opposition from members of the Geography and the Education Departments. Harlan H. Barrows, the chair of the Department of
Geography, denounced the enterprise as intellectually unwise, as a
danger to specialization, and as ignoring the importance of students
learning sufficient facts before they were invited to begin generalizations.[99] From the Department of Education came an even more strident
reaction. Professor Henry C. Morrison was so disturbed by the syllabus
of the new course that he sent a five-page letter insisting that it be

Hermann Schlesinger and Anton Carlson that departmental science courses be
folded into the New Plan curriculum. See the undated letter from late January
1931, marked "Saturday," in the Mortimer Adler Papers, box 56.

98. "Minutes of the Faculty of the Humanities Division," December 3, 1930,
1, and March 12, 1931, 1; Shailer Mathews to Chauncey Boucher, May 9,
1931, Dean of the College Records, 1923–1958, box 7, folder 2.

99. "Minute of the Executive Committee, Division of the Social Sciences," February 23, 1931, Division of the Social Sciences Records, box 17; and "Minutes
of the Department of History," January 24, 1931, 1, Department of History
Papers, box 19, folder 4. Barrows had written to Boucher a month earlier in the
same vein. See Barrows to Boucher, January 21, 1931, Presidents' Papers, 1925–
1945, box 19, folder 9.

dropped from the curriculum.[100] In the first place Morrison was upset with what he called the course's "unscientific point of view," by which he meant that the instructors made no effort to teach the students a set of formal principles by which they might comprehend the social world. Morrison was convinced that "they do not propose to teach the truth, but rather the results of the *a priori* and empirical thinking which happens to be in style....They propose to launch freshmen forthwith into studies which would perhaps be appropriate in advanced university courses." Morrison gamely insisted that if the Division of the Social Sciences "has no principles to teach, it should release the freshmen to the other science divisions, which do have principles." Moreover, allowing students to discuss original documents cold, with no set principles to guide them, was pedagogically irresponsible. Morrison viewed this as the equivalent of "setting people to expressing opinions about pneumonia, typhoid fever, infantile paralysis and sleeping sickness, who are quite innocent of any comprehension whatever of the underlying medical sciences." Finally, Morrison predicted that the course would be a waste of time for the majority of students, whom he dismissed as being mere "confirmed lesson learners." Still other students would be confused, bewildered, and discouraged. A final and larger group of students, who were "cocky and opinionated," would end by becoming "mere intellectual and moral anarchists," suffering from "distinct neurotic degeneration."

In fact, Henry Morrison was correct in that the new Social Sciences course made no attempt to instill a body of principles in the students. Rather than imposing a set of fixed "principles," Gideonse, Kerwin, and Wirth preferred that their students learn empirically the merits of conflicting theoretical approaches by reading and discussing an array of

100. Morrison to Filbey, August 20, 1931, Dean of the College Records, 1923–1958, box 8, folder 2.

original documents and sources. Gideonse himself was dismissive of attempts to create a single social science, based on fixed principles. The instructors consciously refused to tell the students what they should think, since that was, ultimately, a responsibility of the students themselves. As Gideonse later put it, "if there is one duty that could be singled out as the primary one for a college instructor in the social sciences, it would be to cultivate a gingerly attitude against easy generalizations and uninformed efforts to build 'systems'."[101]

Notwithstanding Morrison's acerbic commentary about the Social Sciences course, and resistance from other departmental loyalists who feared a possible loss of their ability to attract first-year students to their own programs, the New Plan survey courses were launched in October 1931. For the most part each course began smoothly and in a well-organized fashion. Given the pace and work load demanded by the new courses, which exceeded anything in the University's undergraduate programs in the past, it was not surprising that during the first year some students found the readings heavy going and the pace of work intimidating, so much so that Boucher was forced to write to the course leaders reporting frequent "complaints of students that they are overworked to the point of serious discouragement."[102] He reminded the course chairs that each course was supposed to require about ten hours of work each week outside of class, and pointedly urged the faculty to "avoid everything that smacks of competition between courses for a lion's share of the student's time." Finally, although he admitted that there might be a small number of students for whom the New Plan was over their heads,

101. Gideonse to Brumbaugh, October 31, 1935, 7.

102. Boucher to M. C. Coulter et al., October 30, 1931, Dean of the College Records, 1923–1958, box 6, folder 8.

the course leaders should remind the students that with diligent work most of them would easily be able to master the material and pass the comprehensive examinations. The dean of Rockefeller Chapel, Charles W. Gilkey, encountered ambivalent responses when he surveyed 450 first-year College students in small groups during the autumn quarter of 1933. Gilkey found that the academic seriousness and dedication of the New Plan students was striking: "There is less interest in under-graduate life, more serious concern about technical and academic phases of the University experiences in which they are situated....Administration and 'old guard' [student] activity leaders should not be surprised at the ever increasing influence of such students upon the extracurricular and fraternity branches of the campus picture." But he also encountered serious complaints about how difficult students found the transition from their high schools to the fast-paced rigor of the new general-education courses in the College: "There is very definite feeling that, for the best of students, the transition from high school atmospheres and methods of study to the University campus and its new plan is a difficult one, and there is not enough instruction and guidance as to methods of study for the new student."[103] In February 1932 Boucher followed with another missive, urging that when the syllabi were revised, the number and amount of readings should be reduced, since "we seem to have erred very definitely on the side of too heavy a load for the average student."[104] Still, over time the courses attracted enthusiastic student constituencies, and the stronger academic quality of the students admitted after 1931 may have

103. The results of these sessions were summarized in Warren E. Thompson, "A Report of the Nine Informal Freshman Discussion Groups at the Gilkey Home, Fall Quarter, 1933," Dean of the College Records, 1923–1958, box 2, folder 14.

104. Boucher to Schevill et al., February 5, 1932, Dean of the College Records, 1923–1958, box 6, folder 8.

played a role in making the courses more sustainable. Students liked the balance between lecture and discussion and the emphasis on reading original documents; and their teachers found it challenging and stimulating.

Faculty ingenuity was able to respond to many of the initial adjustment problems, but often at the cost of creating other problems. For example, in the biological sciences, Merle Coulter found that "the transition from high school to our College was quite a shock to a good many students. The methods and total setting were so different that these students remained in a state of confusion of several months before settling down to a systematic, business-like attack upon their course of work. By that time they had become fairly well oriented but were in need of a review of the subject matter content of the first few months." Coulter responded by organizing regular "review sessions," which became so popular that they were organized throughout the year and which "flourished increasingly" over the 1930s. But Coulter soon realized that the sessions were flourishing too much, since they led students to cut their regular discussion meetings and attend the review sessions, which quickly became known as "cram" sessions for the comprehensive. Having substituted one problem for another, Coulter then restructured the review sessions so that they did not provide a comprehensive overview of the course, but only responded to particular, ad hoc problems generally faced by the weakest students. This put an end to the cramming culture associated with the Biological Sciences general course, or at least deprived it of some of its oxygen.[105]

The Physical Sciences course developed creative interventions to bring students in contact with the actual practice of science. Given the large numbers of students, it was not feasible to plan small-group labs, but

105. Coulter, "Report on Ten Years of Experience with the Introductory General Course in the Biological Sciences," October 1941, 24–26.

Lemon and Schlesinger instead created permanent demonstrations in the form of a Physics Museum, a Chemistry Museum, and a Geology Museum, with demonstration lectures for astronomy at the Adler Planetarium. Lemon was particularly entrepreneurial in new visual materials. Developed in cooperation with the Museum of Science and Industry the Physics Museum consisted of three rooms of about 3,000 square feet in Belfield Hall housing 125 experiments and exhibits which were self-operating or student operated.[106] The purpose of the museum was to expose students to a series of physics experiments in mechanics, heat, wave motion, sound, and light, beginning with the most simple and proceeding to the more complex. Lemon believed that the museums netted the University considerable positive publicity and urged Boucher to see if the College could obtain what he shrewdly called "special consideration" from the central administration for sponsoring these exhibits.[107] Like Coulter, Lemon also developed several motion pictures for use in this course, which supplemented regular lectures, and which afforded students the chance to return to demonstrations and experiments already studied and watch the course of an experiment attain a natural conclusion. Giving students the opportunity to review and restudy the critical stages of a key experiment about which they might be initially unclear would reveal to them the painstaking methods that scientists had to employ to understand more fully the contingent nature of their evidence.

Chauncey Boucher's hope that a more rigorous curriculum would attract smarter and more able students also came to fruition. By the spring

106. See Harvey B. Lemon, "The Physics Museum of the University of Chicago and Its Relation to the New Curriculum," *American Journal of Physics* 2 (1934): 10–17.

107. See "Science Museum Exhibits Tried Out on Students," *Chicago Tribune*, December 4, 1932, 16.

of 1932 University Examiner Louis Thurstone reported to Boucher: "it seems quite certain that we are attracting brighter students under the New Plan than the Old Plan. The exact reason for this may not be evident, but it is probably associated with the publicity for the New Plan."[108] The challenges of the New Plan attracted many gifted students, and Boucher developed a long list of stories that he regularly recited about the gifted nature of his students in the College.

Among the younger faculty, the discussion leaders found themselves caught up in the work and they liked it. Bill Halperin, later a distinguished historian of modern Europe who as a young man taught one of the discussion sections of the Social Sciences general course, reported:

> Many of the students were surprisingly alert and sophisticated, and at times the discussions were extremely suggestive and outspoken....A very considerable number of the students have responded to the challenge by developing very excellent study habits. It is my impression that the New Plan students not only do more work than their old-plan predecessors, but approach their academic problems with greater alertness and understanding. The necessity of integrating and synthesizing data garnered from various fields of learning has provided the more intelligent and industrious students with that intellectual experience which, under existing educational conditions, to a large extent is reserved for post-graduate study.[109]

108. Thurstone to Boucher, March 18, 1932, as well as "General Course: First Year Examination, Autumn Quarter 1931," Dean of the College Records, 1923–1958, box 15, folder 9.

109. Halperin to Boucher, May 27, 1933, ibid., box 8, folder 2.

Similarly, Mary Gilson commented on the excitement of teaching in such an open-ended course:

> Surely no one can criticize the New Plan for regimenting or routinizing the instructor. On the contrary, it furnishes rich opportunities for initiative and experimentation, and no instructor can justly attribute to it any contribution toward a tendency on his part to go stale. In other words, dry rot may attack any instructor under any scheme, but the New Plan has in it potent antitoxins for counteracting such germs.[110]

Equally positive reactions were evident among those teaching in the Humanities general course. Eugene Anderson liked the increased responsibility that fell to discussion leaders in such a wide-ranging and at times unfocused course:

> Since these students are so very young and immature the discussion leader has to make his material popular and he has to do better teaching than he has ever done. This is a point to emphasize—that it is the most difficult teaching, for there is no opportunity to play the taskmaster, you have to win your students and hold them just by the excellence of instruction and not by compulsion. This whole system puts a whole lot more responsibility on the teacher than any other one that I have ever taught under.[111]

110. Gilson to Boucher, April 28, 1933, ibid.

111. Anderson to Boucher, May 22, 1933, ibid., box 7, folder 2.

Similarly, James Cate praised the collegiality and open-mindedness of his colleagues, especially the senior scholars who led the course:

> In many ways I consider our personnel an ideal one. It would be hard to assemble a more congenial group, or one composed of men more eager to shoulder each his part of the load. There is no lack of differences of opinion, and some of our best measures have come as the result of heated discussions, yet once a general policy is laid down there is no refusal to cooperate on the part of dissident minorities. From the point of view of a junior member of the staff, perhaps the most pleasant feature of all has been the attitude of the various heads—Messrs. Schevill, Scott, and Lovett. There is no doubt in any case as to who is in charge of the course, but there is never any intimation of administrative or academic superiority. We younger members have been made to feel from the beginning that the Humanities is very much our course, and I think the result has been a general loyalty and a deeper interest in the work.[112]

Three years later Cate wrote that the combination of lecture and discussion, and particularly the focus on selected texts for more intensive interrogation,

> widened the student's range of interest and have taught him where to go for the great classics and how to read them, projected each against its own age; if we have done this without undue distortion of the ground covered too rapidly, then we feel amply repaid for our efforts. My own opinion is that the Humanities Survey helps

112. Cate to Boucher, June 7, 1933, ibid.

most students more than it harms them; more I would not say about any course.[113]

In June 1933 Harry Gideonse was asked by Chauncey Boucher to evaluate the Social Sciences course after its first two years.[114] Gideonse thought that the course had proven itself successful on several different fronts. In the most basic terms, the course generated high attendance at its lectures, even though they were not mandatory. The course also inspired students to question existing social conditions and it enhanced their interest in discussing contemporary social problems. Gideonse found that most of his students demonstrated "active interest and spontaneous participation" and continued to ask for more discussion of "current social phenomena around them." Because the course was part of a shared and common matrix of expectations that all students had to meet, the course also helped create what Gideonse characterized as "a significant universe of discourse in our student body." The methodology of the course—the interrogation of conflicting original sources—was beneficial because it trained students to uncover the intellectual premises that governed the work of the various authors they read. Gideonse noted, "the other day one of my colleagues informed me that he was convinced that our present organization was one continuous process of indoctrination. What he meant to say was that he felt greater difficulty in presenting his particular type of social theory to students who had followed our particular course of training, because we had stressed in considerable detail the nature and presuppositions upon which his particular theory

113. James L. Cate, "An Introductory General Course in the Humanities," *The Social Studies* 27 (1936): 157–64, here 164.

114. Gideonse to Boucher, June 9, 1933, Dean of the College Records, 1923–1958, ibid., box 6, folder 8.

is based." In other words, inviting students to read original works and think about the preconceptions and presuppositions that they contained was bound to be productively disruptive down the line.

Gideonse did believe that challenges lay ahead for the divisions to adjust the kinds of upper-level courses they would offer students coming out of the general-education program, since many faculty members were unused to interacting actively with students. He also reminded Boucher that if other universities were to adopt Chicago-like general-education courses—which Boucher fondly hoped would happen—it had to be emphasized that the success of the New Plan was very much owing to the innovation, flexibility, and dedication of the new teachers, and not just to new curricular structures and materials: "The new plan is not only a question of method, it is a matter of men and women. During the last two years we have had a remarkable change in the personnel teaching in the College courses in the Social Sciences. That is as worthy of stress as the change in the methods of instruction." This point was to be of crucial significance for the future of the general-education tradition at Chicago, and we will return to it later in this essay.

Gideonse was particularly proud that the New Plan had recruited a "higher caliber of students" and that those students found the Social Sciences course among the most challenging. Whereas in the 1920s social-science courses were seen as "snap" courses, they now rivaled or even surpassed their counterparts from the other divisions in terms of the difficulty of mastering the material presented.[115]

The natural scientists were equally pleased. Merle Coulter was proud that in his course the lectures were very effective: "most of the lecturers were imbued at the start with a strong desire to cooperate in our

115. "Sub-Committee on Curriculum," January 14, 1935, Division of the Social Sciences Records, box 16, 2–3.

educational experiment; and most of them later discovered a substantial satisfaction in presenting their ideas to the large and rather appreciate audience of high-grade young Americans that they found in our course." Coulter also stressed that his colleagues had made a strong effort not to overwhelm students with so many technical terms so that they would fail to "master and apply" the seminal ideas of modern biology. He characterized this strategy as one of "detechnicalization."[116] The Biology course employed as discussion leaders only young postdoctoral fellows, and it tried to select men with research ambitions who would find a home in the relevant department. The faculty associated with the course also produced a number of high-quality textbooks that supplemented the general syllabus.[117]

After two years of teaching the Physical Sciences general course, Harvey Lemon found student "esprit de corps" high, and he defended the policy of having many different lecturers as made necessary by the "great sweep and wide diversity of technical subject matter covered." In fact, Lemon believed the rotation of lectures among different faculty "supplies a frequent freshening of interest that is beneficial and in my judgment more than offsets the distinct disadvantage of this method, which produces a certain lack of unified technique of presentation and consequent unavoidable necessity on the part of the student to make

116. Coulter, "Report on Ten Years of Experience with the Introductory General Course in the Biological Sciences," October 1941, 8, 10.

117. Ralph Buchsbaum, *Animals without Backbones* (Chicago, 1938), A. J. Carlson and V. Johnson, *The Machinery of the Body* (Chicago, 1937), Fay-Cooper Cole, *The Long Road* (Baltimore, 1933), M. C. Coulter, *The Story of the Plant Kingdom* (Chicago, 1935), H. Garrett, *Great Experiments in Psychology* (New York, 1930), H. H. Newman, *Evolution, Genetics, and Eugenics* (Chicago, 1932), and A. S. Romer, *Man and the Vertebrates* (Chicago, 1933).

readjustments and to sometimes indulge in inevitable invidious comparisons."[118] Discussion and large-group review sections were reasonably well attended and pedagogically effective, and Lemon noted of one of his colleague's reactions: "Dr. Bretz who was the most ardent objector of large group discussions…expressed himself as astonished and delighted a few weeks ago when over 150 students participated with him in one of the most stimulating and eager discussion groups which it has ever been the writer's privilege to witness." In general, in light of the fact that much of the material of the course was analytic rather than descriptive, and that the majority of students had no intention of pursing advanced studies in science, Lemon believed that his course had made a "creditable showing," in that students scored well on the final comprehensives and voluntary quizzes. He later asserted:

We know that no inconsiderable number of our able students have been, and are, progressing through [the New Plan] with the utmost satisfaction and joy. This fact alone would seem not only to justify the experiment to date but to encourage the further attempt to carry it along and improve upon it. Indeed we know of no one who has been intimately associated with this work, either in our own or other divisions, who does not seem to share in a greater or less degree this general conviction.[119]

118. Harvey B. Lemon, "Report on the First Five Quarters of the General Course in the Physical Sciences," May 1933, Dean of the College Records, 1923–1958, box 8, folder 1.

119. Harvey B. Lemon and Hermann I. Schlesinger, "After Five Years: An Appraisal of The Introductory General Course in the Physical Sciences," Dean of the College Records, 1923–1958, box 8, folder 1.

The impact of the New Plan's general-education courses on the quality of our student body was momentous. A study undertaken in 1940 indicated that more students were completing their BA degree programs in nine quarters or less than had done so before 1930. More important was the academic quality of the students and the impact that they had on campus student culture. Chauncey Boucher argued strongly in 1935 that the New Plan had seen a significant upgrading in the quality of the students: "Though we did not raise our entrance requirements, we hoped that the announcement of the New Plan would attract a larger number of superior students. This hope has been realized. We have more applicants for admission than ever before from students who ranked in the top tenth of their graduating classes in excellent preparatory and high schools." This improvement in high-school rankings was paralleled by significant increases in aptitude of matriculating students, as measured by the American Council on Education's Psychological Examination, which was administered to all entering first-year students. The median score achieved in 1933 was 38.5 percent higher than that achieved by Chicago students entering between 1928 and 1930.[120] Indeed, by 1934 University of Chicago students ranked third in the nation in aptitude for educational achievement out of 240 colleges and universities who participated in the examination.[121]

Given the enhanced aptitude of matriculating students, it was also not surprising that most New Plan students felt positive about their educational experiences in the demanding new curriculum. A survey of 1,065 New Plan alumni in 1938–39 who had completed the College

120. Boucher, *The Chicago College Plan*, 110.

121. "Facts about Undergraduates at the University of Chicago," Dean of the College Records, 1923–1958, box 15, folder 2.

between 1931 and 1935 revealed that a great majority were either very satisfied or satisfied with the quality of teaching that they experienced at Chicago and that they were equally satisfied with what they had learned in their general-education courses in the College. When asked "should every student be required to take the [general-education] survey courses?" almost 89 percent answered affirmatively. The young alumni were equally convinced (72 percent) that the instructional materials of the general-education courses were well organized and that they got a lot out of the courses in which they participated (73 percent). Seventy-eight percent of the alumni believed that the New Plan curriculum gave them a greater satisfaction in living their lives. And, not surprisingly, almost 88 percent answered yes to the question, "did you like the freedom allowed under the New Plan?"[122]

Of course from the distance of ninety years, it is difficult to apply the kinds of fine-grained evaluation mechanisms that we would use today. Still, the slow acceleration of time to degree and the generally favorable image that the University clearly had in the eyes of these students suggest that Chauncey Boucher's gamble of 1930–31—that a more challenging and difficult curriculum but also one that was more coherently organized and efficiently taught would lead to more gifted students enrolling in the University—was proven correct.

But the impact of the New Plan was also evident in the external operations of the College. The collapse of big-time football in the late

122. "Students at the University of Chicago," 1940–1941, 7–8, ibid. See also the "Report of an Evaluation of the College Program of the University of Chicago by Students Who Entered the College in the Autumn Quarters of 1933, 1934, and 1935," ibid., box 9, folder 12. This survey has comparative evaluative data from 648 students on student satisfaction with the four general-education survey courses. Of the four, the Biological Sciences course was by far the most popular.

1930s was attributed by many to the fact that the College was now recruiting more academically oriented students, which lowered the competitive athletic position of Chicago within the Big Ten: "there have rarely been, in recent years, more than two or three Maroon regulars who could make the second or third teams at other Big Ten Schools."[123] Robin Lester concluded that "the New Plan, adopted in 1931, resulted in a brighter, more critical student body and one much less likely to have participated in athletics at secondary school or on the Midway."[124] The New Plan did privilege sturdier and more resilient students, as Bill Halperin confirmed when he observed that "the greatest praise for the New Plan invariably comes from the superior students, while the sharpest criticism emanates from those who find it very difficult to adapt themselves to the novel features of the present arrangement."[125]

The educational impact of the new general-education courses on student culture went beyond the classroom to encourage what Walter Laves described as

the inter-stimulation of a large group which goes through the same study at the same time. It has been fun to watch the spread of a new term or idea throughout the whole group via lectures, dormitory discussions, small informal and formal group "sessions", and so forth, with the echo, in the form of questions or disputes that arise in these discussions, coming back to the faculty. The common

123. Quoted in Robin Lester, *Stagg's University: The Rise, Decline, and Fall of Big-Time Football at Chicago* (Urbana, 1995), 183.

124. Ibid., 173.

125. Halperin to Boucher, May 27, 1933, 4, Dean of the College Records, 1923–1958, box 8, folder 2.

and cumulative building up of a field of reference or universe of discourse was never as obvious under the old plan, the effort was more scattered, students could not take it for granted that their classmates were interested in the same notions and as a consequence study was not nearly as obviously a major activity as it now seems likely to become.[126]

Laves, who had been an undergraduate student at Chicago between 1919 and 1923 and thus knew the pre–New Plan curriculum personally, described a revolutionary side effect of the general courses—namely, that they helped create a powerful group consciousness among undergraduate students, all of whom were now involved in deeply challenging collective experiences. To the extent that the University of Chicago came to have a distinctive and intensely self-conscious academic culture in the twentieth century, this factor was of enormous import.

The initial success of the New Plan did not preclude certain operational problems, and these became clearer as the years wore on. The comprehensive exams generated divergent and sometimes questionable practices involving tutors. Some students sought "extra" help in prepping for the exams, which often amounted to circumventing the need for attending lectures. Issues of conflict of interest soon arose, as to whether those individuals associated with the courses and who had a role in the formulation of the exams should also be permitted to tutor students for extra compensation. Boucher was firm in his opposition to such practices, but the very existence of such "off-shore"" practices highlighted

126. Walter Laves, "Report on the First Year of the Introductory Course in the Social Sciences," 13–14.

the reservations of those who opposed the comprehensive exams on other grounds.[127]

Even among the faculty teaching the courses some reservations emerged. The younger instructors canvassed in 1933 pointed to serious problems, particularly lack of coherence in the lectures, unevenness in student preparation to cope with fast-paced courses requiring huge amounts of reading, occasional student confusion over the "big picture" that the courses were trying to convey, lack of coordination among the four survey courses, unevenness in the success of the discussion groups, and great frustration with the comprehensive exams, which many instructors felt required too much of their time to construct and which failed to measure adequately the achievement of the students.

Arthur P. Scott complained as early as 1933 that "partly as a result of the pressure of time to finish the syllabi in short order, the four courses were prepared with virtually no consultation between the four committees in charge."[128] Similarly, Louis Wirth was concerned with the fact that the founders of the four courses had not "arrived at any fundamental consensus as to our notion of general education. Individually and in a sort of formal way we have expressed ourselves on this subject. We have not been able to 'sell' our ideas to one another and cannot therefore be very effective in 'selling' them to the world at large, not to speak of our students."[129]

127. Boucher to Louis L. Thurstone, June 8, 1935, Dean of the College Records, 1923–1958, box 6, folder 2.

128. Scott to Boucher, November 1, 1933, ibid., box 7, folder 2.

129. Wirth to Hutchins, September 13, 1935, Presidents' Papers, 1925–1945, box 19, folder 4.

Worries about overload and heavy reading assignments that were too schematic and superficial were also troublesome. Ferdinand Schevill complained to Boucher about the danger of overwork that was built into the New Plan, and he suggested on several occasions that the reading load of the new Humanities course was too heavy. He also worried about its all-too-inclusive quality, urging that some restrictions on the range of topics and more focus on whole books would be desirable.[130] Lest Scott take this as a concession to Robert Hutchins, Schevill added candidly, "you may say that I am raising the President's cry against the pouring out of mere facts and in favor of directive concepts. I have less reason for denying the impeachment as I have taken essentially the same position for the larger part of my teaching career and have certainly represented it from the first in my discussions with you."[131] Scott too wanted the College to provide the Humanities course with more resources, so that the number of lectures could be reduced and the discussion sections increased, but he received little support for his requests.[132]

Tensions with the departments were also evident, as department chairmen tried to influence the appointment of discussion leaders who would be assigned to the general courses. In 1932 Ferdinand Schevill

130. Boucher to Schevill and Scott, May 27, 1932, and Schevill to Boucher, June 16, 1932, Dean of the College Records, 1923–1958, box 7, folder 2

131. "I think our range of subject matter is so excessive as to be unmanageable; and I crave restriction, precision, and definiteness in place of the loose, illogical encyclopedism now in practice." Schevill to Scott, May 12, 1934, Dean of the College Records, 1923–1958, box 7, folder 2.

132. See Brumbaugh to Scott, April 29, 1938, ibid. Brumbaugh admitted that Scott had "raised the question several times with reference to increasing the number of discussion periods and reducing the number of lectures in Humanities I." Brumbaugh was either unable or unwilling to support these requests.

threatened to resign in protest over what he felt to be William Dodd's unauthorized meddling in the teaching roster for the Humanities course.[133] Boucher talked Schevill out of it, but the incident highlighted the political fragility in which the new courses operated, and the latent structural tensions between the College's interests and those of the departments.

The new system of comprehensives also encountered resistance. Harvey Lemon thought that the examiner's office manifested a lack of "creative critical helpfulness" to the faculty of the general courses, relying too much on faculty initiative and manifesting "too little initiative and drive."[134] Walter H. Laves laconically opined: "The comprehensive examinations have been the most disputed part of the new program as far as our course is concerned. The preparation of questions has taken more time than any other feature of the new arrangements. In the minds of most of those concerned with the course the results have *not* corresponded with the effort. Judging by conversations with our colleagues in parallel courses these impressions are not limited to our group." Laves added, "it is difficult for an inexperienced group like the Board of Examiners to realize just how much work and time the faculty has to put into such a task."[135]

Over time, faculty also became unhappy with the failure of some students to show up for lectures and discussion sections, even though

133. Schevill to Boucher, May 26, 1932 and Boucher to Schevill, May 27, 1932, Dean of the College Records, 1923–1958, box 7, folder 2.

134. "Report on the First Five Quarters of the General Course in the Physical Sciences," 12, Dean of the College Records, 1923–1958, box 8, folder 1.

135. Walter H. Laves, "Report on the First Year of the Introductory Course in the Social Sciences," 4, 9. Dean of the College Records, 1923–1958, box 8, folder 2.

these were, in theory, voluntary and not mandatory. Given the high professionalism of the faculty and their investment of time to prepare their lectures and discussions, it was understandable they might become irritated if some students treated their efforts in a cavalier manner.[136] By 1936 Harvey Lemon and Hermann Schlesinger had become sufficiently disillusioned with student attempts to game the system by picking and choosing which lectures they would attend and which materials they would read in order to pass the final comprehensive exams that they recommended that no student should be allowed to sit for a final comprehensive unless he or she had passed successfully the three quarterly examinations that were embedded as advisory instruments in the structure of the Physical Sciences general course.[137] Although Lemon and Schlesinger continued to pay lip service to the idea of final comprehensive examinations, their proposal was in essence a strong, if oblique, criticism of a key behavioral premise of the New Plan, namely, that students should have perfect freedom to prepare for their comprehensive exams in whatever way seemed most appropriate to them.

The unhappiness of faculty with students not fully engaging the material and instead cramming for the comprehensives was confirmed by a study in 1939 that found that middle- and lower-ability students who merely audited the survey courses, as opposed to students who participated more fully by taking quarterly exams and quizzes for advisory grades, were likely to score lower on their final comprehensives. This finding, coming just before the outbreak of World War II, suggested that class attendance and focus on the material discussed in class were

136. W. C. Krumbein to Brumbaugh, November 5, 1936, Dean of the College Records, 1923–1958, box 6, folder 9.

137. Lemon and Schlesinger, "After Five Years: An Appraisal of The Introductory General Course in the Physical Sciences," 11.

important, especially for students who were ranked in the middle or lower echelons of academic ability. Today we would take the idea that the personal interaction between faculty and students is a vital and constitutive part of learning and that the classroom work of teachers does matter as obvious and self-evident, but at the time it seemed to undercut the rhetoric of freedom that was at the foundation of Boucher's original New Plan design from 1931.[138]

Changes in the staffs of the graduate students and young faculty who served as discussion leaders also posed challenges, since each staff was bound to experience comings and goings. In November 1936 Aaron Brumbaugh broached the idea of creating half-time internships for apprentice discussion leaders so that they might become familiar with the courses.[139] In the spring of 1939 Brumbaugh then asked the directors of the general courses to provide written statements of the purposes and objectives of each of their courses.[140] This latter request reflected the impact of Ralph Tyler's appointment as the university examiner in 1938. Tyler wanted the general-education staffs to design examinations that reflected and supported each course's synoptic learning goals, which would allow the exams to measure the achievement of students in terms of the purposes and objectives of the course.[141] Tyler's theoretical aims

138. "The Achievement in Comprehensive Examinations of Students Who Received 'R' in Quarterly Reports Compared with Students Who Received Qualitative Quarterly Marks," Summer 1939, Dean of the College Records, 1923–1958, box 15, folder 2.

139. See his proposal from November 1936 in ibid., box 6, folder 9.

140. A. J. Brumbaugh to P. H. Boynton et al., March 16, 1939, Dean of the College Records, 1923–1958, box 6, folder 9.

141. Interview of Benjamin Bloom with Christopher Kimball, April 14, 1986, 22; June 4, 1986, 41; February 5, 1987, 77–80, Oral History Program. See, also

may have been salutary, but the fact that the staffs were now compelled to generate detailed statements about the goals of their courses was a sign that the initial rush of ad hoc experimentation was slowing down and that more systematic forms of institutionalization were needed in order for the general-education program to sustain itself. This trend raised the longer-term issue of whether new instructors joining the courses in the future would share the same values and same aspirations as the original architects. The creation of guidelines for "in-service" procedures in 1941 to ensure proper training and socialization of new staff members was also a sign of such institutionalization.[142] Both processes accentuated and compelled the more formal development of staffs qua staffs, which by the later 1940s even had official charters and rules of procedure. The curricular upheavals of 1942–46 resulted in even more sophisticated and self-conscious attempts on the part of the general-education staffs to articulate the pedagogical and methodological goals of each of their courses, so that they could be scrutinized and debated by faculty from other fields.[143] This in turn led to shared modes of

Bloom, "Changing Conceptions of Examining at the University of Chicago," 304–10; and "The Construction and Use of Examinations in the College of the University of Chicago: A Statement by the University Examiner," February 9, 1950, Dean of the College Records, 1923–1958, Series 98–41, box 99.

142. "The In-Service Training of Staff Members in the Introductory General Courses and English 102 in the College Division," May 12, 1941, Dean of the College Records, 1923–1958, box 6, folder 9. This document summarized the individual statements sent to Brumbaugh in February 1941 by Merle Coulter, Arthur Scott, R. J. Stephenson, Walter Laves, and Percy Boynton (English composition).

143. An early example of this genre is the seventeen page memorandum, "Relationships Among Social Sciences 1, Social Sciences 2, and Social Sciences 3," 1946–1947, Dean of the College Records, 1923–1958, box 8, folder 2.

educational discourse about the goals and objectives of the College's general-education program as a whole, a body of discourses that, more than anything else, gave an aura of distinctiveness to the Hutchins College at its zenith between 1947 and 1954.

WIDER CHALLENGES AND OPPORTUNITIES OF THE NEW PLAN

The New Plan's impact on the wider instructional culture of the University can be illustrated by examining its relationship to the Division of the Social Sciences and to the School of Business. A particularly thorny issue emerged in the Division of the Social Sciences relating to the kind of baccalaureate program that social-science majors would complete in order to qualify for a BA degree after they finished the College's two-year general-education curriculum. In 1931 the divisional faculty had decided that a student who wished to obtain a BA degree had to take at least five of seven possible introductory courses, each representing one of the Social Sciences' departments, and to sit for a comprehensive examination assembled from questions drawn from these courses. In addition, the student had to specialize in a single subject as a major field of study and to take six other upper-level courses in the division as free electives. The departmentally based introductory courses, each bearing the generic number of 201, were mounted in a hodgepodge fashion in 1932. Within three years considerable unhappiness had emerged about the value of these courses, and in late 1934 the divisional dean, Robert Redfield, appointed an ad hoc subcommittee on the divisional curriculum to investigate the effectiveness of the 201 courses, their relationship to the

wider domain of undergraduate education in the Social Sciences, and
their relationship to the New Plan's general-education sequences. As
Redfield explained to Hutchins, he hoped that the ad hoc committee
might undertake a "thorough review of the curriculum of the Division
and make recommendations for changes." Redfield was frustrated: "at
present the student is confronted with a list of courses, which vary enor-
mously in character, and some of which are plain fakes." In addition to
the 201 courses, Redfield also hoped that the committee would survey
departmental course offerings more generally, with a goal of determining
"which of them represent frontiers of science and scholarship on which
the man giving the course is operating, and which of them represent
substantially 'canned' material."[144] Ideally, Redfield also wanted the
departments to decide what they were trying to accomplish with their
courses, and to say so publicly, so that the students would be able to
make more informed decisions about which courses to take.

For over a year Herbert Blumer, Charles Judd, Frank Knight, Frederick Schuman, and Redfield labored to understand how best to teach
social sciences to third- and fourth-year undergraduates. The subcommittee heard, almost as a grand jury, testimony from an array of
influential historians and social scientists. Fay-Cooper Cole of the
Department of Anthropology argued that integration was already a
stated goal of the Social Sciences general course in the College, and that
the interrelationships among the social sciences could be better articulated there than in more advanced courses. Cole also attacked several of
the sacred cows of the New Plan, insisting that students now were more
likely to work less than ten years previously, because they were not compelled to attend class and take course-based examinations. For Cole the

144. Redfield to Hutchins, November 12, 1934, Division of the Social Sciences
Records, box 16.

new comprehensive-examination system had encouraged bad study habits by allowing the student too much independence from conventional instruction: "under the old system students were encouraged to do independent work through term papers; now they are encouraged only to pass examinations." Cole wanted the comprehensive exams to be based on the actual courses that faculty taught, not the courses upon the final comprehensive exams.[145]

The next witness was Harry Gideonse, who defended the integrating principle that informed the Social Sciences I course (the nature of contemporary society under the impact of rapid industrialization), and who also had a rather low opinion of the 201 courses, which he felt were simply a rehash of general materials already covered effectively in the College's general-education sequences. Gideonse argued that students should be required to take at most three (instead of five) of the 201 courses, spending more of their time on genuinely specialized courses where they could engage in specialized work. In strong contrast to Cole, Gideonse believed that the New Plan students were both brighter and harder working than students from the 1920s. Finally, Gideonse mentioned that he did support a great works of social science honors course that sought to integrate multiple perspectives on doing social science, but insisted that this was most appropriate for seniors, not for freshmen, thus implicitly rebuking Hutchins's and Adler's venture with first-year students.[146]

Like Gideonse, Louis Wirth defended the integrated nature of the Social Sciences general course, which was not a combination of three

145. "Report of the Sub-Committee on Curriculum," December 17, 1934, 1–11, Division of the Social Sciences Records, box 16.

146. "Sub-Committee on Curriculum," January 14, 1935, 1–9, ibid.

disciplines, but rather used disciplinary material from all of the social sciences. At the same time Wirth was not fully satisfied with the general course, since he "hoped that over-emphasis on examinations could be minimized in order to improve student morale and to encourage intensive work with zest, interest and spontaneity." Because the College faced serious budget restrictions, it was forced to overburden the members of its teaching staffs. Wirth also worried about the dangers of over organization for the faculty themselves, insisting that the individual instructors might be discouraged by having to follow a standardized syllabus, which "destroys spontaneity and cramps teaching style." And like Gideonse, Wirth had a low opinion of the 201 courses, which "let down" the students because of their "disparate, isolated" structures and "make shift" qualities.[147]

William Hutchinson represented the views of the historians, and his comments were more akin to Cole's. Hutchinson's discussion revolved around the College general-education sequences as much as it did the division's 201 courses. Hutchinson thought that the "old plan" of undergraduate studies was deservedly dead and buried and that the New Plan had brought Chicago students who were "more alert, broader, more willing to challenge lecturers and books, more critical and resilient." At the same time these same students were only interested in learning generalizations, not facts, which led the students to have "a large amount of intellectual arrogance" for which they needed "to be taught some humility." Hutchinson blamed "the general courses in the College, where whole civilizations are set up and knocked down within a few days,

147. "Sub-Committee on Curriculum," January 23, 1935, 1–9, ibid.

although the College denies this charge. Students are interested in studying the past only as a series of problems, without reference to time, space
and background."[148] Another critical problem was that the New Plan
"actually squeezes out the teacher. With syllabi, optional class attendance, etc., the teacher is reduced in status, becomes merely a walking
bibliography."

There was broad agreement on the part of all interviewed that, as
Louis Wirth put it, "as they now stand our 201 courses fail to synthesize
the social subject matter of the social sciences and probably cannot be
sufficiently modified (as long as they are given by separate departments)
to satisfy the need for a well-articulated and integrated general training
in the social sciences."[149] Wirth's statement begged the question of
whether the faculty could actually imagine and agree upon a common
set of assumptions as to what constituted nondepartmentally based social
sciences. The challenge of imagining how one might "integrate" social
sciences via interdisciplinary or comparative coursework for College
juniors and seniors then preoccupied the committee, and resulted in
numerous memoranda and position papers for and against.

The debates in the committee itself were vigorous. The discussions
inevitably ranged over a wide array of not very related topics, from the
quality of high-school teaching in the United States to the quality of
text books used in secondary education to duplication of courses among
related departments to the quality of lecturing that was done by the
divisional faculty to the time that faculty had to do research (Charles
Merriam insisted that the University did not need to have sabbaticals
since "every year is a sabbatical year for anyone who wishes to do

148. "Sub-Committee on Curriculum," January 29, 1935, 6, ibid.

149. Wirth to Redfield, undated [January 1935], ibid.

research") to the alleged mixture of ideology and politics that was now afflicting secondary school education.[150]

But the specific issue that was the originating point of the committee —the future of the seven 201 courses—resulted in little consensus. Some, like Charles Judd, disliked the whole arrangement, arguing that the generalizing work of such courses ought to be done in the College and not the division, and wanted them abolished. Fay-Cooper Cole, in contrast, thought that the College was not in a position to provide such systematic introduction to multiple disciplines, which could only be done by the departments. Robert Redfield believed that the division did have the responsibility for creating interdisciplinary courses in comparative social science on a higher level than could or should be done in the College. Using the image of the divisional curriculum as a "pyramid involving gradual and progressive specialization," he proposed in March 1935 a scheme of six new courses that might replace the departmentally based 201 courses.[151] These courses were to include Social Life: Its Nature and Setting, a study of the biological roots of human nature and behavior, the human habitat, and the social and cognitive structure of human behavior; A Comparative Study of Culture Types, a study of the structure of literate and nonliterate cultures and societies in the contemporary world; History and Social Science, a review of the historical perspective and of basic types of historical methodology, including those used in archaeology and prehistory, as well as types of historical interpretation and the functions of history; Statistics in the Social Sciences, an introduction to quantification in the social sciences, including statistical concepts, measurement, sampling, probability, and correlations; and a

150. "Sub-Committee on Curriculum," February 4, 1935, ibid.

151. "Sub-Committee on Curriculum," March 11, 1935, ibid.

two-quarter course on Social Science and Social Action, a discussion of
basic concepts of political science and economics, focusing on democratic government as a mode of social choice, state direction in a
free-market economy, the role of education and pressure groups in influ-
encing changes in social attitudes, and the types of group behavior
resulting from conflicting social and economic interests.[152] Redfield
believed that the division had the responsibility to continue the work of
general education begun in the College, but on a higher and more sophisticated level, focusing on the multiple ways that the individual disciplines
confronted common social issues and phenomena. He also believed that
it was a responsibility of the University of Chicago to show leadership
in American higher education and research and to do more than merely
"perpetuate the conventional division of labor in the social sciences field
and preserve the departmental presentations of subject-matter."[153]

Redfield's proposed new courses would move toward the idea of an
integrated social science by a series of pincer-like interventions. His program was in fact a brilliant conceptual attempt to do two things at once.
He hoped to continue the revolutionary curricular élan of the early
1930s, but on a higher level, by providing more transparent interdisciplinary pathways from the new general education of the College to the
hyper-specialization of the departments. He also hoped to create a greater
sense of supra-departmental consciousness within the division itself,
making the division more than a series of isolated and mutually distrust-
ing political units. Redfield's courses were to be created by volunteers
drawn from different departments, and students wishing to major in the

152. See the draft in Redfield to the Members of the Sub-Committee, August
27, 1935, ibid.

153. Memorandum of Robert Redfield, December 10, 1935, ibid.

social sciences would be required to take all six courses and a common
final examination that would be "genuinely integrated" in drawing from
the materials of all of the courses. Fittingly, Robert Hutchins found
Redfield's proposals to "mark a great advance over the 201 courses. I beg
to offer my congratulations to the Dean and the committee."[154]

Yet Hutchins's congratulations were premature. When Redfield submitted his proposals to the faculty of the departments, he encountered
both active and passive resistance.[155] This was particularly the case in
Political Science where Quincy Wright, Frederick L. Schuman, and
Jerome Kerwin wrote trenchant commentaries on Redfield's proposals.
Wright, who was the most senior, was also the most negative. He insisted
that the integration of the social sciences was a virtual phantom that was
both meaningless and dangerous unless a student had first mastered the
individual scholarly disciplines. For Wright the proper function of an
undergraduate curriculum was to encourage differentiation and not
integration.[156] Frederick Schuman in contrast thought that to postpone
such integrative work to graduate school—which is essentially what
Wright proposed—was to consign it to oblivion, since graduate programs were inevitably even more specialized. Schuman also argued that
the current individual disciplines of the social sciences were products of
a nineteenth-century political and social imagination in which economics never impinged on politics and where social issues were kept strongly
apart from the state and its scientific sponsorship. For Schuman the

154. Hutchins to Redfield, October 16, 1935, ibid.

155. See the comments reported in "Sub-Committee on Curriculum," December 11, 1935, ibid.

156. "Comments on the Recommendation of the Sub-Committee on
Curriculum Created by the Executive Committee of the Division of the Social
Sciences," ibid.

contemporary world of the 1930s showed how antiquated this compart-
mentalization of the social sciences had become—politics could no
longer be written in ignorance of economics or sociology, for example.
If Chicago were serious about teaching a truly modern perspective on
the social sciences, it would have to develop curricular modes that represented the scrambled quality of the world of knowledge and action.[157]
Jerome Kerwin sided with Wright, urging that the departments offer
seven to eight disciplinary courses that would "acquaint the student with
the standards of criticism toward observations of social phenomena and
concepts about social phenomena employed by the most advanced contemporary social sciences." Although these courses would reflect upon
general questions, they would be controlled and staffed by the individual
departments, which was in effect, a return to the status quo.[158]

Nor did Redfield's proposal gain unalloyed support from the College,
since Gideonse and Wirth, representing the College, insisted that much
of what Redfield's committee wanted to achieve was already present in
the existing Social Sciences general course.[159] In the end, Redfield
encountered disharmony from the various departments, where uncertainty reigned about who would teach these new courses and whether
they would lead to a lower profile, perhaps invisibility, for their particular
departments. Facing what Charles Judd called "the phenomenon of
mutual interdepartmental distrust" among the various departments,

157. "Comments on the Memorandum of October 28, 1935 Submitted by
Professor Quincy Wright in Commentary on the Recommendation of the Divisional Subcommittee on Curriculum," ibid.

158. "Memorandum in Organization of Undergraduate Work in the Social Sciences," October 28, 1935, ibid.

159. "Sub-Committee on Curriculum," May 6, 1935, ibid.

Redfield settled for a modest compromise.[160] The existing departmental 201 courses were left in place, but he was authorized to encourage the experimental creation of a few more boldly interdisciplinary ventures that would highlight the "general underlying importance of the fields selected to all students in the social sciences....The selection and organization would not be dictated by departmental interests or follow strict departmental lines."[161] Redfield hoped that these new courses would "make a tremendous contribution to the progress of Social Science and put the Division far ahead of any other institution in this field."[162] However this proved to be little more than face-saving, since none of the new experimental courses were mounted before the coming of the war. After the recentering of the BA degree in early 1942, which eliminated any role for the departments in Chicago's undergraduate curriculum, the effort was structurally less compelling in any event. In the end, Redfield wrote ruefully, if also humorously to Hutchins, "the stirrings as to curriculum in this Division are nothing to shout about. The mountain labored and brought forth a few grasshoppers."[163] The failure of Redfield's plan must have been a clear sign to Hutchins that Charles Judd was correct in arguing that both the departments and the faculty associated with the 1931 general-education courses stood in an unholy alliance. It might be said that the path toward the radical decision that Hutchins took in 1942—which essentially stripped the departments of any role

160. "Sub-Committee on Curriculum," December 11, 1935, ibid.

161. "Sub-Committee on Curriculum," March 5, 1936; "Report of the Sub-committee on Curriculum, Division of the Social Sciences," March 9, 1936, ibid.

162. "Sub-Committee on Curriculum," August 13, 1935, ibid.

163. Redfield to Hutchins, July 15, 1936, ibid.

in undergraduate education at Chicago—was more clearly marked out after the failure of Redfield's scheme of 1935–36.

If the Division of the Social Sciences struggled to exploit the efficacy of the New Plan and to connect it in innovative ways to more specialized domains of knowledge, the School of Business found that Boucher's new general-education program provided an ideal solution to serious educational problems it had faced for over a decade. It is a little remembered fact that from 1898 until 1946 the University had an undergraduate business major, becoming by 1914 "a leader in collegiate education for business" and developing a curriculum that "had a profound influence on programs of collegiate training throughout the United States."[164] In 1932 the School of Commerce and Administration (renamed the School of Business in the same year) had 211 undergraduate students, compared with 55 graduate students, and the tuition income of the undergraduates was by far the largest share of unrestricted revenue available to the school.[165] After a hiatus of seven years, the College and the Graduate School of Business established the Professional Option program in 1953, under which College students could double count the first year of the school's MBA curriculum for their senior year in the College.[166] For most of our institutional history, therefore, we have offered interested College

164. "Business Training and Research," July 1930, 1, Presidents' Papers, 1925–1945, box 110, folder 6.

165. In the autumn quarter 1932 undergraduates paid $23,888 in tuition as opposed to $4,166 by the graduate students. "A Comparative Statement of Tuition in the School of Business, Autumn Quarter 1931 and Autumn Quarter, 1932," Presidents' Papers, 1925–1945, box 110, folder 4.

166. This was accomplished by the Faculty of the College agreeing in late December 1953 to accept nine courses from the Graduate School of Business as counting toward a baccalaureate degree, thus recreating a system that offered a (de facto) business program for College students.

students the possibility of an undergraduate business program. The University's long experience with professional education was strengthened by the creation of the New Plan, since after 1931 a primary requirement for the admission of Chicago students to the school's business major became the completion of the New Plan's general-education courses. The School of Commerce and Administration had hoped as early as the mid 1920s to more sharply demarcate the boundary between liberal-arts general education in the first two years of college, and the more specialized studies, which students could pursue in the field of commerce in the second two years.[167] It wanted to base itself on "general education as administered in secondary schools and junior colleges." In 1926 the school decided to abandon instruction in the first two years of undergraduate life to the liberal-arts colleges of the University.[168] The creation of a separate college in 1930 and the New Plan curriculum in 1931 thus came at exactly the right moment for the school, which renamed itself as the School of Business in 1932 and announced that its educational purview would be focused on the final two years of undergraduate education and an additional year that would lead to a master's degree.[169] The school's faculty believed that future businessmen and women had to be exposed to a rigorous introduction to the major fields of the liberal arts via the New Plan's general-education courses, especially courses in the social, biological, and physical sciences, which the school deemed particularly important "in view of the highly inter-dependent character of

167. W. H. Spencer, "Memorandum on Business Training and Research at the University of Chicago," 1930, 9–11, Presidents' Papers, 1925–1945, box 110, folder 4.

168. L. C. Marshall to Max Mason, June 26, 1926, ibid., box 101, folder 10.

169. See Floyd W. Reeves, W. E. Peik, and John Dale Russell, *Instructional Problems in the University* (Chicago, 1933), 134–35.

modern society in which business is carried on."[170] As early as 1926 the former dean of the School of Commerce, Leon C. Marshall, had argued: "when the education of business executives is broadly conceived, antagonism between vocational education and liberal education disappears.... Vocational education for the task of the business executive includes and must include liberal education."[171] Two years later Marshall insisted, "let us accept the attitude that 'general education' should never be thought of as something which has been 'completed'; and let us agree that a true professional school is vitally concerned with both 'general education' and 'social values'."[172] Marshall's thinking about business education was greatly influenced by his work on the University committee chaired by Chauncey Boucher in 1928 that produced the first report calling for a radical reform of undergraduate education at Chicago, including the creation of a serious program of general education.[173] Marshall's ideas had a strong impact on his colleagues. As Professor Wesley N. Mitchell of the school put it in 1939,

> from the very beginning of this development in collegiate education,
> the School of Business has assumed its full share of responsibility

170. "Business Training and Research," July 1930, 9–10, Presidents' Papers, 1925–1945, box 110, folder 10.

171. Leon C. Marshall, "The Collegiate School of Business at Erehwon," *Journal of Political Economy* 34 (1926): 298–99. More generally, see Leon C. Marshall, ed., *The Collegiate School of Business: Its Status at the Close of the First Quarter of the Twentieth Century* (Chicago, 1928), esp. 3–44, 189–203.

172. Leon C. Marshall, "A University School of Business," in *The Collegiate School of Business,* 199.

173. "Report of the Senate Committee on the Undergraduate Colleges," May 7, 1928, Dean of the College Records, 1923–1958, box 27, folder 6.

for elevating standards of business education. The program of the School is designed to develop initiative, independence, and resourcefulness among its students. It places emphasis upon a sense of relationships, upon effective habits of work, and upon ability to analyze and solve problems....Through analysis of business situations and problems it endeavors to train students to think effectively and consistently about these problems and to form valid business judgments.[174]

As a result of the curricular connection between the newly created College and the School of Business, throughout the 1930s and early 1940s hundreds of students transferred to the school after completing their general-education curriculum in the College and graduated with a BA degree in business. Unlike the case of the Social Sciences, the School of Business had no desire to create additional intermediary structures between general and more specialized education. For the School of Business the New Plan thus provided a perfect transition point that justified the operation of a more focused and analytically grounded curriculum of business education for advanced undergraduates.

174. Wesley N. Mitchell to Emery Filbey, November 30, 1939, Presidents' Papers, 1925–1945, box 110, folder 4.

COLLISIONS AT THE TOP: ROBERT HUTCHINS AND THE CRITIQUE OF THE NEW PLAN

 erhaps the greatest challenge faced by the New Plan program was that the new president, Robert Maynard Hutchins, felt substantial ambivalence toward it and toward several of its leaders. It is one of the great ironies of our history that Hutchins—the man usually associated with the founding of the Core—came to dislike the general-education courses that Boucher's teams had put together, and that so many of the leaders of these courses became ardent opponents of Hutchins's leadership as time went on. Maynard Krueger, who as a young instructor in the 1930s had witnessed Hutchins's covert criticisms of the New Plan at firsthand, later recalled, "the new College [curriculum of 1930–31] had been initiated before Hutchins ever got hold of it, and it was not being planned on the basis of which Hutchins would have preferred." According to Krueger, Hutchins's connection with Mortimer Adler in 1930 already predisposed him toward a "heavy emphasis on the Great Books." Hutchins "would have preferred that from the very beginning...[the curriculum] be[come] what he did make a great effort to make it later, but at the time, the people who were doing that reorganizing were not Hutchins's preferred people."[175]

Beginning in the autumn of 1930, Robert Hutchins had indeed collaborated with a young, brash, and highly controversial scholar from Columbia University, Mortimer Adler, in organizing a great-books

175. Interview of Maynard Krueger with Christopher Kimball, May 11, 1988, 3, Oral History Program.

honors course each quarter over a two-year cycle. Modeled on a similar course taught at Columbia University by John Erskine, the seminar was called General Honors 110 (in 1934 it was renamed Classics of the Western World), and in the first year it assigned extensive readings from the work of Homer, Herodotus, Thucydides, Aristophanes, Plato, Aristotle, Cicero, Vergil, Plutarch, Marcus Aurelius, the New Testament, St. Augustine, Thomas Aquinas, Dante, Cervantes, and other worthies. (The second year then ran from Duns Scotus to Freud.)[176] The course met two hours a week on Tuesday evenings, with no formal lectures, and enrolled twenty freshmen, the students being responsible for doing all of the assigned reading for each class. Their evaluation consisted of an oral exam, administered by outside examiners, as well as an essay exam based on the analysis of selected quotes. The reactions of the outside examiners were very positive, with Richard McKeon of Columbia University suggesting in 1932 that "to judge by the examinations of the sixteen students who appeared before me, I can think of no more effective course in collegiate education than that which resulted in the training of those students." Similarly, Stringfellow Barr of the University of Virginia observed that "I can hardly overstate my admiration for the intellectual poise with which your students have taken hold."[177] The College Curriculum Committee eventually voted to allow students to use the final examination in this course as a substitute for one of the elective sequences beyond the general-education survey courses that each Chicago undergraduate was required to take under the New Plan.

176. The list of readings for the General Honors course is in Presidents' Papers, 1925–1945, box 38, folder 5.

177. McKeon to Hutchins, June 12, 1932 and Barr to Hutchins, June 15, 1931, ibid.

Mortimer Adler's arrival on campus had hardly been fortuitous, since Hutchins's failed attempt to impose him (as well as Scott Buchanan of the University of Virginia) during the 1929–30 academic year on the Department of Philosophy as an associate professor was a political disaster.[178] By early 1931, when Chauncey Boucher was organizing the teams to plan the new general-education courses, he wrote candidly to Hutchins: "nearly every day I encounter an expression of distrust or fear regarding the selection of men to be put in charge of the four general divisional courses provided in the report of the Curriculum Committee—namely, that Mr. Adler will be put in charge of the Humanities course, and that others of his ilk will be brought in for the other courses. In each instance I think I have convinced the person that such fears are unwarranted."[179] Little did Boucher know what lay ahead.

Adler proved a potent influence on Hutchins. They had first met in 1927 when Hutchins was at Yale Law School and he engaged Adler on a project in the study of the logic of evidence in the law on the recommendation of the British philosopher C. K. Ogden.[180] Adler's first book,

178. The events were described in detail in "A Statement from The Department of Philosophy," [1930], Presidents' Papers, 1925–1945, box 106, folder 14. See also Amy A. Kass, "Radical Conservatives for Liberal Education" (Phd diss., Johns Hopkins University, 1973), 108–18; and Hutchins to Adler, November 11, 1929, December 4, 1929, and January 30, 1930, Adler Papers, box 56. McKeon's name was also on the list, making up what Hutchins called the "holy trinity." Ibid., January 30, 1930. Adler later provided his own account of the fiasco in his *Philosopher at Large: An Intellectual Autobiography* (New York, 1977), 129–30, 145–48.

179. Boucher to Hutchins, March 3, 1931, Presidents' Papers, 1925–1945, box 106, folder 14.

180. Adler, *Philosopher at Large*, 107–10; Mary Ann Dzuback, *Robert M. Hutchins: Portrait of an Educator* (Chicago, 1991), 88–108.

Dialectic, was about to be published under Ogden's auspices. This book, and many of Adler's other writings of the 1930s, already have the encyclopedic and Aristotelian character that later became identified as Adler's Thomism.[181] *Dialectic* ranges over the history of Western philosophy in pursuit of a taxonomic ordering of kinds of inquiry. Adler claimed: "Dialectic is a convenient technical name for the kind of thinking which takes place when human beings enter into dispute....It is presented here as a methodology significantly different from the procedure of the empirical scientist or...the mathematician. It is an intellectual process in which all men engage in so far as they undertake to be critical of their own opinions, or the opinions of others."[182] Adler distinguishes throughout the book between theoretical sciences (the traditional branches of philosophy) and the modern empirical sciences. He thinks of his inquiry as identifying an overarching methodology for all science since "in so far as any science achieves theoretical form, its universe of discourse has dialectical structure."[183] As early as 1927, then, Adler was trying to provide a theoretical framework for the kinds of discussions that were already taking place in Erskine's General Honors course at Columbia. His philosophical writings at Chicago and his teaching with Hutchins carry this work forward, and Hutchins's later juxtaposition of theoretical ideas (which were good) against empirical facts (which were not) flowed directly from the influence of Adler's conceptual frameworks. It is

181. For example, *What Man Has Made of Man* (New York, 1937), a series of lectures on philosophical psychology, and "An Analysis of the Kinds of Knowledge" (1935), an outline of epistemology ranging from Aristotle and Euclid through Galileo and Newton to modern empirical social science, which was circulated in mimeograph through the University of Chicago Bookstore.

182. Mortimer Adler, *Dialectic* (New York, 1927), v.

183. Ibid., 239.

natural that Adler was drawn to the work of St. Thomas Aquinas, since Thomas's *Summae* provide a model for both the encyclopedic treatment of philosophical problems and the engagement with all accessible traditional learning that Adler found attractive.[184] In Adler Hutchins found a man nearly his own age who possessed substantial learning, contentious eloquence, and profound intellectual ambition. It was a natural collaboration. Both men aspired to traditional philosophical learning of great seriousness and scope, and both men, for better or worse, aspired to remake the institutions of the University in the pursuit of that ideal.

The Adler-Hutchins great-books course, which Adler conceived as a radical alternative to the kind of curriculum that Chauncey Boucher had instituted in 1931, was one ongoing challenge to the New Plan. Indeed, the glowing evaluations about his great-books course that Hutchins received from men like McKeon and Barr must have had a powerful impact in motivating him to think beyond the curricular structures of the New Plan. A second challenge came forward in 1933 in the person of Ronald Crane, a respected professor of English who initiated discussions in the autumn of 1933 about restructuring the curriculum in a way that would privilege humanistic courses at the expense of the natural sciences.[185] Crane also generated considerable controversy in the spring of 1934 by writing a memorandum impugning the intellectual ambitions of the Department of History. The memorandum arose from a specific set of issues unrelated to the New Plan—the decision of the Department of History to associate itself with the Division of the Social

184. Adler makes the case for linking his work with Aquinas's in his 1938 Aquinas Lecture at Marquette University, *Saint Thomas and the Gentiles* (Milwaukee, 1938).

185. See John W. Boyer, *Three Views of Continuity and Change at the University of Chicago* (Chicago, 1999), 50–53.

Sciences for administrative purposes in January 1933, which caused considerable unhappiness among faculty in the Humanities.[186] One of Crane's arguments was about the need for greater clarity as to who was responsible for history and who in fact was a historian: "it has come to be widely assumed among professional historians that their proper domain is coextensive with the history of culture or civilization, and that they ought to give increasing attention in their teaching and writing to subject matters, such as economics, philosophy, science, and even art which are already organized elsewhere in the University as special historical disciplines." In Crane's mind, social and political history were the legitimate province of the "professional historians," but other domains of historical inquiry and teaching should properly be left to experts in the relevant substantive fields. Since History was Chauncey Boucher's home department, and since two prominent historians— Ferdinand Schevill and Arthur Scott—were the primary leaders of the Humanities general course that explicitly sought to go beyond political and social history to include literature, art, and philosophy, Crane's intervention could also be seen as a further covert challenge to Boucher and the New Plan.[187]

186. "Minutes of the Department of History, January 13, 1933," Department of History Records, box 19, folder 6; "Minutes of the University Senate," March 11, 1933.

187. R. S. Crane, "The Organization of History in a University," April 1934, and the Department of History's response "The Objectives of a Department of History," June 1934, are filed in ibid., box 25, folder 3. In his response to Crane's report Boucher cleverly urged that the conditions that Crane identified should lead History to urge its graduate students to take more courses in specialty departments, not less, and thus gain greater professional preparation to order do history of a broad interdisciplinary nature. See Boucher to H. F. Mac-Nair, May 4, 1934, ibid.

As his contacts with Adler and Crane grew more intense, Hutchins drifted away from whatever superficial commitment to the New Plan he had had in 1931. This shift is apparent in Hutchins's confidential report to the Board of Trustees in early 1935, where he observed of the New Plan that

> only the four general courses can be called attempts to give a general education. They are barely half the ordinary student's work. The rest of his time he spends in specialization, which by the legislation is the task of the Divisions, and in "tool" subjects, which he should take only if he is going on into the Divisions. The curriculum is seriously over weighted on the side of the natural sciences. Two divisions of natural science are necessary for administrative purposes; it does not follow that two natural science courses are necessary for a general education. A serious result is that the Fine Arts are squeezed out or almost out of the curriculum....The curriculum would be much better if there were a general course in the natural sciences, the social sciences, the fine arts, philosophy, and history. The difficulties with such an arrangement are (1) that we have no adequate staff in the fine arts and (2) it might be hard to get those who teach the present courses to vote to change them. The whole course of study suffers greatly from a disease that afflicts all college teaching in America, the information disease. I have never favored survey courses in the usual sense. A hasty look at all the facts in a given field does not seem very useful from any but a conversational point of view. I hoped that the general courses would deal with the leading ideas in the various fields of knowledge. Although some progress has been made in this direction, the great weakness of the curriculum is still its emphasis on current information.

Hutchins then continued: "I believe that departmental courses of all kinds should be excluded from a general education. I am sure, too, that a college course which is based largely on the reading of great books, with lectures on them and discussions of them, is more likely to produce understanding, even of the contemporary world, than a vast mass of current data."[188]

These tensions came to a head in 1934 and 1935, when the New Plan sustained a series of public collisions, the like of which the University had never before experienced, at least in the case of undergraduate education. At the December Convocation of the University in late 1933 Robert Hutchins opened a rhetorical battlefront by denouncing those who would inundate the young with facts as opposed to concepts in undergraduate teaching: "the gadgeteers and the data-collectors, masquerading as scientists, have threatened to become the supreme chieftains of the scholarly world." In contrast, the University should really be a "center of rational thought," which was the "only basis of education and research." The current system of education was unfortunately designed "to pour facts into the student with splendid disregard of the certainty that he will forget them, that they may not be facts by the time he graduates, and that he won't know what to do with them if they are....The three worst words in education are 'character', 'personality', and 'facts'. Facts are the core of an anti-intellectual curriculum." Instead of collecting evidence, the "gaze of the University should be turned toward ideas," which would "promote understanding of the nature of the world and of man."[189] Hutchins continued this theme in early January 1934 at the

188. *Report of the President, 1930–1934,* February 1, 1935, 21–22.

189. The speech garnered the attention of the local press. See Edgar Ansel Mowrer, "Hutchins Stirs University by Questioning Science as a Basis for Philosophy," *Chicago Daily News,* December 27, 1933, 5.

annual trustee-faculty dinner where he insisted, "I have attempted to show that facts are not science and that the collection of facts will not make a science; that scientific research, therefore, cannot consist of the accumulation of data alone; that the anti-intellectual account of science given by scientists has produced unfortunate effects on the work of other disciplines which wished to be scientific; and that our anti-intellectual scheme of education, resulting in large part from this anti-intellectual account, was misconceived and incapable of accomplishing the objects set for it by its sponsors." He further attacked those university teachers who "offend us in filling their students full of facts, in putting them through countless measurements, in multiplying their courses, in insisting that they must have more of the students's time so that they can give him more information."[190] Hutchins's discursive framework—"ideas" as being more important than "facts" and learning more important than memorizing—was highly simplistic and betrayed a fundamental misunderstanding about the way in which modern scientific research was conducted, but it afforded a fascinating stance with which to take the moral high ground, accusing universities of a thoughtless disregard for the truly essential features of the mission of liberal education.

Hutchins's discursive bravado, which could be read as targeting either the New Plan courses directly or at least impugning the curricular imagination of the faculty who had organized them, gave encouragement to the then editor of the *Maroon*, a young undergraduate by the name of John Barden, to launch a frontal assault on the New Plan. Barden was a New Plan student with a relatively modest academic record (he had

190. Both speeches were later published in Robert M. Hutchins, *No Friendly Voice* (Chicago, 1936), 24–40.

received Cs in his comprehensive exams).[191] Barden had met Mortimer
Adler when he audited the Adler-Hutchins General Honors course and
also enrolled in the autumn of 1933 in Adler's class on Law in Western
European Intellectual History. Barden quickly fell under Adler's intellectual sway.[192]

In early January 1934 Barden wrote an editorial in which he slammed
Chauncey Boucher's New Plan curriculum as purveying facts and not
ideas: "if we assume that a general education does consist of a collection
of ideas rather than a collection of facts, the new plan is not administer-
ing a general education."[193] Barden continued this theme in weekly
commentaries throughout the winter and spring quarters of 1934.
Barden's critiques of the New Plan as providing facts and not ideas might
be said to have the appearance of farce, given the heavy theoretical
superstructures offered by Gideonse et al., but his real target seems to
have been the New Plan's basic assumption that scholarly professionalism
and current research should inform the teaching of general education.
He seemed to have a clear bias against the natural sciences and against
the structure of the comprehensive exams that tested a student's mastery
of such research. In a subsequent essay, in the form of a dialogue between
Socrates and Exercon on the ideal of the University, Barden portrayed
Socrates as arguing with refined irony that "many people believe that
general education consists of exposition of the latest results of modern

191. Frank H. Knight to Walter B. Smith, December 7, 1934, Frank H. Knight
Papers, box 62, folder 2.

192. See Barden's use of the Adler-Hutchins great-books course as a model for
a future curriculum in the College in the *Chicago Maroon*, March 8, 1934, 2.
For Adler's subsequent account of these events, see his *Philosopher at Large*,
149–90.

193. *Chicago Maroon*, January 5, 1934, 2.

research."[194] Barden also attacked the New Plan lectures as mainly recounting facts that could easily be obtained in textbooks.[195] Instead of teaching "great" general ideas, based on original sources that were presumably easily accessible to an undergraduate, the faculty were presenting highly technical courses based on advanced research in which students were overwhelmed with empirical data before any larger syntheses could be offered.

Within a month of Barden's initial attacks and Hutchins's speeches, the student biology club Alpha Zeta Beta invited Mortimer Alder and Anton J. Carlson to a public debate in Mandel Hall before seven hundred students on February 9, 1934, on the theme of facts versus ideas. This uproarious event consisted of Carlson taking the stage and reading a series of propositions defending the scientific method, followed by Adler's witty and ironic replies, which defended Hutchins's ideas as coherent and reasonable and, by implication, criticized Carlson's presentation as an example of the obfuscations of a kind of scientific research that seemed to deny the importance of conceptual abstractions in the articulation of the scientific method.[196]

194. Ibid., January 9, 1934, 2.

195. Ibid., February 20, 1934, 2.

196. Ibid., February 9, 1934, 1. Carlson had denounced Hutchins's views in a newspaper interview in late December 1933, insisting, "the particularly disturbing element in the present instance is that it comes from the president of a university whose main distinction has come from its achievements in science." Gifford Ernest, "Fact-Finding of Science Defended by Dr. Carlson; Denies Charges of Hutchins," *Chicago Daily News*, December 28, 1933, 8. Adler's notes for the February 1934 debate are in the Adler Papers, box 57.

Emboldened by Adler's rhetorical brinksmanship, Barden commissioned four College seniors to write critiques of the four general survey
courses in March 1934, based on their published syllabi. Because they
had matriculated in 1930, the four essay writers were studying under the
requirements of the old curriculum, and none of them had actually taken
any of the New Plan's general-education courses. What they had in
common was that all four had been students in the Adler-Hutchins great-
books class, which in effect had become a rival general-education course
based on very different intellectual principles. Janet Kalven attacked the
Humanities course as being a course in intellectual history offered by
nonphilosophers, when, to her mind, only philosophers were competent
to undertake such an assignment. Kalven claimed to find many "offenses
against sound scholarship" in the organization of the course. Particularly
offensive for Kalven was the syllabus's cavalier treatment of Plato and
Aristotle, which suggested that there were important differences between
the thought of these two philosophers, where Kalven insisted they were
tightly bound by similar theories of man and reason. In all, the Humanities syllabus was "sophistical, dogmatic, anti intellectual, inaccurate,
misleading, inconsistent, sentimental, and slovenly." James Martin criticized the Social Sciences course as being filled with covert ideas of
Comtean positivism, the theoretical structure of which he proceeded to
critique. Ignoring most of the actual material taught in the course,
Martin then opined that the course as a whole was based on "bad scholarship." Darwin Anderson thought that the Physical Sciences course
suffered from too heavy a reliance on evolutionary theory and "mechanistic" theories of the origins of the universe and urged that the course
spend more time investigating the "fundamental principles of natural
philosophy." Finally, Clarice Anderson attacked the Biological Sciences
course as having a "mechanistic bias" and as being too dependent on

evolutionary frameworks, and then spent the rest of her essay explicating Aristotle's theory of human nature and its relevance for modern science.[197]

The four critiques were gratuitous, poorly argued, and naive, and other College students who were enrolled in the New Plan courses quickly mounted a counteroffensive.[198] One such pro–New Plan student, Marie Berger, gathered 250 signatures on a petition accusing Barden of conducting an authoritarian crusade that was divorced from the majority of student opinion. Berger pointed out that the four writers had no exposure to the courses they were writing about with such animus, and that this was an unfair method by which to proceed.[199]

The attacks in the *Maroon* clearly got under Chauncey Boucher's skin. Boucher thought that Barden was a "smart aleck" who had demonstrated "bad taste." Stunned by the negative publicity generated by the *Maroon*, Boucher had the College Curriculum Committee issue a memorandum denouncing the recent criticisms of the New Plan as the work of "rationalistic absolutism which brings with it an atmosphere of intolerance of liberal, scientific, and democratic attitudes" that was "incompatible with the ideal of a community of scholars and students recognizable as the University of Chicago."[200] Upon receiving a copy of this statement, Barden wrote an ironic, but deeply insulting, letter to Boucher, wondering why Boucher would have taken the views of students in the *Maroon* so seriously and adding, "I don't care how good or bad a college news-

197. Ibid., March 8, 1934, 1, 3, 5–6.

198. Ibid., April 11, 1934, 1–4

199. Ibid., March 14, 1934, 2.

200. "The Educational Objectives of the College in the University of Chicago," April 21, 1934, Presidents' Papers, 1925–1945, box 19a, folder 3.

paper may be, it is *never* worth official notice by any division of the faculty. I feel that the College faculty have immeasurably degraded themselves by officially recognizing *The Daily Maroon* even exists."[201] What Barden failed to appreciate, of course, was that Boucher's real worry was that Robert Hutchins not only agreed with the attacks, but that Adler and he had encouraged the students to press them.

The debate about facts versus ideas had a fascinating afterwash among the faculty from the Department of Economics. Harry Gideonse kept a poster board outside his office in Cobb Hall filled with clippings from the *Maroon*, to which he added derisive commentaries and which were available for students to see. More importantly, Gideonse submitted a commentary to the *Maroon* in June 1934 asserting that Adler and his followers were "pathic and pathetic" in their search for "certainty" in knowledge and values, presenting themselves as a group of "tired young men [who] are rejecting the tentative groping for truth that is character-istic of modern science."[202] Frank H. Knight, who was a voluble and assertive personality and not easily intimidated, also entered the fray with a strident attack on Adler's alleged medievalism, accusing those who would attack modern thought (like, presumably, Mortimer Adler and Robert Hutchins) of engaging in "absolutistic verbalism," "'wish-thinking' as a substitute for truth," and "intellectual dictatorship." Throwing Thomism in the same class of "isms" as Marxism, Knight insisted that both were "social reform propaganda," and that "neither society nor any group or class in it can be an intellectual community unless we begin with an overwhelming presumption against the

201. Barden to Boucher, May 3, 1934, Adler Papers, box 56.

202. Harry D. Gideonse, "The New War of Science and Dogma," *Chicago Maroon*, June 7, 1934, 2.

soundness of any teaching whose promoters cannot place themselves above suspicion of motivation by other interests than love of truth and right. Between advocating and truth-seeking, meaning the quest of right answers to problems, there is a nearly *impassable* gulf."[203]

After trying to publish his broadside "Is Modern Thought Anti-Intellectual?" in the *Maroon*, where Barden torpedoed it, Knight sent it in samizdat fashion to various key faculty leaders around campus.[204] He sent it to Chauncey Boucher with the comment, "the very sources of intellectual integrity are being systematically poisoned in the University as a whole....Of course we cannot be absolutely sure how far the President is backing the rankest kind of empty and bigoted verbalism and encouragement to dogmatism on the part of the most incompetent, but the evidence seems to me overwhelmingly for conviction....It seems to me impossible to believe that the President is not consciously conniving at, if not deliberately pushing, the whole uproar."[205] Chauncey Boucher responded, "I *know* how much real genius the College Faculty members have shown in the immense amount of work they have done with verve and enthusiasm to design and administer what I know to be the best College program in the country. A Dean who would remain passive and not turn his hand to save this glorious achievement from being wrecked,

203. "Is Modern Thought Anti-Intellectual?" Knight Papers, box 61, folder 22. It was eventually published in *The University of Chicago Magazine*, November 1934, 20–23, with Knight complaining about the *Maroon*'s refusal to print it.

204. "I am sure Adler wouldn't get to first base, or six inches from home plate, if he had to stand on his own feet, but if the President's public utterances and general conduct mean anything at all the thing is a serious menace. If a leading university jumps for medievalism as a cure for the perplexities of modern life and thought, then the human race deserves to be drowned in something besides water." Knight to Beardsley Ruml, June 23, 1934, ibid.

205. Knight to Boucher, July 28, 1934, ibid.

would not be worth the powder to blow him to Hell."[206] Boucher also insisted, "if the Faculty will but stick together and present a nearly united front, they can 'get' any damned Dean or even a President who can be shown to be a nuisance rather than an aid." It says much about how dispiriting the situation had become for the first Core organizers that their putative leader and the real architect of the New Plan, Chauncey Boucher, expressed himself in such strident, but also humiliating terms.

The dispute also found its way into the sanctums of the Department of History, where the historians found themselves on the defensive by the memo written by Ronald Crane. Crane would later turn against Hutchins, but in 1934 he included himself along with Adler and Hutchins as working in common on behalf of "our educational ends."[207] Even before Crane's broadside the nervous chairman of the Department of History, Bernadotte Schmitt, who felt that his department was particularly exposed in the context of Hutchins's attack on fact mongering, circularized his colleagues with a memo arguing that their graduate courses might be seen to be too fact oriented, and urging them to restructure them to be more "interpretative and integrating."[208] Schmitt met with opposition from his fellows, and soon had to back down.[209]

The spring of 1935 then brought a wholly different kind of challenge. The Walgreen Affair has been the subject of another of my essays, and

206. Boucher to Knight, July 31, 1934, ibid.

207. Crane to Adler, July 31, 1934, Adler Papers, box 56.

208. Memorandum of Bernadotte E. Schmitt, January 29, 1934, Department of History Records, box 25, folder 3. Ironically, the kind of courses that Schmitt wanted on the graduate level was already present in Schevill's Humanities general course in the College.

209. William T. Hutchinson Diary, entries of February 14, 1934, and February 19, 1934.

I will not repeat that story here.[210] But it is worth remembering that the context for Lucille Norton's accusations that she had been taught pro-communist doctrines at the College and manipulated to embrace communism was the fact that she was a student in the Social Sciences general course taught by Harry Gideonse. Once her uncle, Charles Walgreen, had made his accusation, and made it publicly, the University community and Robert Hutchins found themselves caught up in the circus-like atmosphere of a Red scare. Walgreen and the Hearst press that manipulated Walgreen tried to tar a number of individuals at the University, but among the central players in the end were Norton's teachers in Social Sciences I, Harry Gideonse and Louis Wirth. Gideonse volunteered to testify before the Illinois Senate Committee investigating the case, and he used his testimony as an opportunity not only to rebut Walgreen's accusations directly—he proudly reported that of the 5,987 pages of reading that a student was expected to do in Social Science I, less than 1 percent had anything to do with communism, and that about three thousand pages were related to American governmental institutions—but he also denounced "the entire trend toward collectivism—whether of a Fascist or Communist sort—with the gravest concern." Gideonse insisted that it was the responsibility of a university to provide its students with opportunities to debate current controversies "in light of established facts and critical scholarship."[211] For anyone familiar with Gideonse's confrontation with Barden the year before, and with Frank Knight's denunciation of intellectual authoritarianism on campus, Gideonse's choice of words would not have been lost on the

210. John W. Boyer, *Academic Freedom and the Modern University: The Experience of the University of Chicago*, rev. ed. (Chicago, 2016), 42–66.

211. Testimony of Harry D. Gideonse, May 24, 1935, 122–29, here 125–26, Laird Bell Papers, box 8, folder 8.

University audience. That Robert Hutchins found himself in the ironically frustrating situation of defending Gideonse's right to teach the *Communist Manifesto*, and that he did so eloquently and unflinchingly, says something about Hutchins's own core values.

The Walgreen controversy preoccupied students in the College and led to various statements which allowed students to mobilize the critical reading and writing skills that they had been taught in the New Plan's survey courses. One young woman who was a friend of Lucille Norton wrote a paper on the affair, entitled "The 'Ism Witch Scare'," in which she insisted that Harry Gideonse was a "self-styled pro-capitalist conservative" who could hardly be accused of purveying communism to Chicago undergraduates. But, in her view, what Gideonse's course did do was to expose students to a range of views about the American political and economic system, which she found healthy:

> If persons in college are not sufficiently mature to think about the possibilities of government other than American, when will they be?...If we cannot think freely, discuss freely, and study freely all manner of social organization or disorganization in the universities where every possible opportunity for finding the truth is made available, where shall we go?...the University does not teach subversive doctrines. They do not advocate an unquestioning acceptance of any principle of government. They are attempting to teach intelligent criticism of government and economic philosophies so that we may more wisely work toward an American Utopia, accepting that which advances the cause, rejecting that which retards.

She concluded by noting, "I hope I have succeeded in conveying the impression that we freshmen are not so immature that we cannot think for ourselves."[212]

Harry Gideonse had played a minor part in the Barden-*Maroon* fiasco, but his role as a leader of the disloyal opposition to Robert Hutchins grew rapidly after 1934. Maynard Krueger later insisted that Gideonse was "the chief vocal leader of an opposition to Hutchins," not in the least because he was respected by the faculty of Physical Sciences and Biological Sciences.[213] He became the preeminent spokesman for what Krueger called the "anti-Hutchins position" on the faculty of the later 1930s.[214] Harry Gideonse was first brought to the attention of the Department of Economics by William Ogburn, who had known him during the years he spent at Columbia University in New York. Gideonse

212. Alda M. Luebbe, "This 'Ism Witch Scare'." Mary Gilson sent a copy of this paper to Aaron Brumbaugh on December 23, 1935, with the comment, "she told me she gave Mr. Walgreen a copy. Not bad for an 18 year old girl, is it?" Dean of the College Records, 1923–1958, box 6, folder 7.

213. Interview of Maynard Krueger with Christopher Kimball, May 25, 1988, 13.

214. "I stayed in close touch with him all the rest of his life. I always thought of him as more nearly an Englishman than an American, despite the fact that I knew he was Dutch. He was on the liberal side of all social economic questions and he regarded what he understood to be the Hutchins position—and what I understood the Hutchins position, also—as a view of educational content that was against the modern and back toward the utterly classical content. While Gideonse, in prescribing reading lists for courses in the College, made some considerable amount of classical formulations, he didn't regard himself as having any intention of becoming a captive of that view. That position of his was very quickly appreciated by the people of rather high standing here in both the Biological and the Physical Sciences....In fact, he was more nearly a spokesman for the anti-Hutchins position than anybody in the Physical or Biological Sciences." Interview of Maynard Krueger with Christopher Kimball, April 28, 1988, 5.

was hired in early 1930 to coordinate the department's undergraduate program, but within a year of his coming he was offered the opportunity to become the coordinator of the College's new Social Sciences general courses created in 1931. Although hired as an associate professor, he was not given a tenured appointment, and this fact soon became crucial in the drama that eventually played itself out. When Gideonse was first proposed for an appointment by the Department of Economics in 1930, then Chair Harry Millis noted: "At twenty-nine he is not a real economist and he may never become an economist of the first rank. He is, however, an excellent teacher, a natural leader, and a real personality. He seems to be able to draw the line neatly between what is good for and effectual with young people, and what is not, and has had interesting and varied experience and background for one of his years....Of course, the appointment of a young man, especially to function as in this case, is more or less of an experiment, and involves a certain amount of risk. It is partly for that reason that I recommend a three-year contract." Hutchins approved the appointment, but with the discouraging proviso, "ok if the Department understands they may be choosing this as [against] a 'great economist'."[215]

In October 1935 Gideonse rejected calls that he and his colleagues make the Social Sciences course more "integrated" and systematic. To Aaron Brumbaugh he pointed out that

> to call a group of related disciplines the division of the *social sciences* does not create *a* social science, any more than the creation of the division of the *humanities* creates *a* humanity. The term "social

215. See Millis to Woodward, January 23, 1930, Presidents' Papers, 1925–1940, Appointments and Budgets, box 25, folder 5.

Harry Gideonse, circa 1935

science" is a mistranslation of the German "sozialwissenschaft" which is correctly translated as "*knowledge* about society" rather than as social *science*. A first year course in social sciences (we call it "introduction to the study of contemporary society" in our syllabus) is therefore not comparable to a first-year course in the physical sciences....I think my colleagues would join me in saying that if at any time any one should be able to persuade a committee chosen from a list of representative members of the Division (say, for instance, Redfield, Merriam, Viner, Ogburn, Millis, Wright, Knight, etc.) of the general validity of any principles of "systematic

social science" not now taught in our College work, we shall cheer-
fully accept their findings and introduce these "principles". As it
stands, "systematic social science" is a figment of uninformed
imagination in so far as it extends beyond the boundaries of what
is now taught in the introductory courses.[216]

Gideonse continued by insisting that "the function of the college is to
teach in the best possible manner the results of the best established
scholarship. It is not its function to teach material that is utterly unac-
ceptable to representative scholarship and in many respects antithetical
to its dominant tendencies."

Nor was Gideonse alone in these views. They were consistently shared
by his colleagues. Maynard Krueger later remembered, "in the social
sciences there was never a time, from the time Harry Gideonse came
here, from the time the staff was organized, when the Great Books would
have got any votes in that staff. Now, that doesn't mean they were against
good books, but it did mean that they did not propose to be captured
by something that they regarded with very great suspicion. The concept
of the Great Books…was a concept that had a great deal of disrespect
amongst members of the faculty."[217]

Gideonse followed his rejoinder to Brumbaugh a year later with an
essay in October 1936 in *Social Studies* where he took up the issue of the
pervasive search for systems of certainty in contemporary intellectual
and political practice, ranging from "the absolutism of fascism to that

216. Gideonse to Brumbaugh, October 31, 1935, 5, Dean of the College
Records, 1923–1958, box 8, folder 2.

217. Interview of Maynard Krueger with Christopher Kimball, May 11, 1988,
30–31.

of communism, and cover[ing] in its broad sweep the curious antics of those who have found a 'Road Back' by retiring to the 'rational order' of Aristotle and St. Thomas of Aquinas." In the context of the American academy Gideonse saw this trend as a kind of radical counterpoint to the destruction of the old classics-based educational system of the nineteenth century. Having given itself over to "freedom of election" the academy now found itself surrounded by those who proffered easy and comfortable solutions to restore holistic order via ideological prescriptions and theoretical syntheses drawn from the distant past. Gideonse did not deny the need for overcoming the disjointedness of modern knowledge, but he insisted that this chaos could only be overcome by embracing modern thought and modern science on their own terms and seeking problem-oriented solutions drawn from the new knowledge of the various disciplines. Rather than training "fixed persons for fixed duties" with incantations of past dogmas, it was the obligation of the modern college to educate flexible minds who would see through the allures and temptations of the "systems." Gideonse argued,

> the clamor for a rational order, for a comprehensive set of first principles with "due subordination" of historical and current empirical material selected with an eye to illustration or confirmation of metaphysics, is essentially a claim to intellectual dictatorship....The tide of increasing specialized knowledge will continue to run, metaphysical or administrative Canutes to the contrary notwithstanding....Our basic problem is not that of improved *means* to unimproved *ends*, but rather that *means* are ever more available to *ends* ever more muddled and evanescent. Philosophy's most tempting opportunity lies in the clarification and statement of the values by which we live, and such a

clarification of values will spring from a detailed and synthetic knowledge of the conditioning means rather than from sterile parroting of the stale metaphysics of the past.[218]

Gideonse also tangled with the powerful chair of the Department of Education (and general supporter of Robert Hutchins), Charles Judd, who denounced the first-year Social Sciences course as taking up "in far too great detail many of the intricate problems of economics" and as conceiving "of the organization of society as determined by the forces which have brought about the Industrial Revolution."[219] Judd believed that Gideonse's essay in *Social Studies* smacked of intolerance of rival views: "You go out of your way, as it seems to me, from time to time to combat the people who have ideas that are not in agreement with your own. I am accustomed to thinking of discussions of the curriculum as objective rather than partisan. I have never been able to understand how some of you who are students of society ignore so completely the social elements which enter into university and school organizations."[220] Gideonse responded angrily: "to me and my colleagues [your] letter was disconcerting evidence of the extent to which even people on our own campus can put forward opinions and statements of fact about the work of their colleagues that have no more relation to reality than the views of some critics of higher education outside the universities."[221] Judd's

218. Harry D. Gideonse, "Integration of the Social Sciences and the Quest for Certainty," *The Social Studies* 27 (1936): 363–72.

219. Charles Judd, "Memorandum on the Curriculum," 4, Division of the Social Sciences Records, box 16.

220. Judd to Gideonse, October 22, 1936, Presidents' Papers, 1925–1945, box 102, folder 2.

221. Gideonse to Judd, November 20, 1936, ibid.

criticism of Gideonse's efforts was part of a larger critique of the New Plan's links to the faculty of the divisions, and the quiet aversion that many New Plan leaders felt toward collaboration with the University High School. In 1937 Judd complained about the "obstructions which have been encountered *all along* in coordinating the instructional program of the new college unit with the work of the lower schools....The College curriculum departs from the ideal curriculum for general education because it is determined in its organization by the fact that the University has four Divisions—an organization which was set up to serve the purposes of specialization of advanced students and the purposes of research. That the divisional organization should reach down and determine general education and control the courses given in the period of general education is a calamity."[222]

Harry Gideonse's trenchant opposition to Robert Hutchins doomed his career at Chicago. By early 1935 Hutchins had decided that he wanted to force Harry Gideonse off the faculty, telling Chauncey Boucher that he had informed Gideonse that he was "not prepared to say that we should increase his salary as the income of the University improves or to assure him that he would be placed on permanent tenure."[223] In the spring of 1936 the Department of Economics sought to make good on their initial commitment to Gideonse that he would be offered tenure and a full professorship and formally recommended such to Hutchins. Hutchins rejected the proposal out of hand. In July 1936 the full professors of the department then sent a respectful but forceful plea to Hutchins to reverse his decision, but Hutchins would

222. Judd to Brumbaugh, June 1,1937, Dean of the College Records, 1923–1958, box 19, folder 7.

223. Hutchins to Boucher, February 23, 1935, Presidents' Papers, 1925–1940, Appointments and Budgets, box 25, folder 8.

not bend. The department insisted that Gideonse had been hired to be a superb teacher of college-level economics and had been assured that distinguished teaching, rather than research, would be the primary qualification used to measure his future advancement and promotions. Now, exactly the opposite had happened, and this from a president who claimed to be interested in quality undergraduate teaching. The writers worried greatly that Hutchins action was motivated by his personal dislike of Gideonse, because of Gideonse's opposition to Hutchins. They strongly hoped that this was not the case:

> Mr. Gideonse's views on educational policies to be followed in the College may have differed in some respects from yours, and, in accordance with the tradition of academic freedom which has always prevailed at the University and to which you have given many magnificent services, he may not have hesitated to express himself on these matters....If the impression should once gain ground that those who freely objected to administrative policies were denied promotion, strong men would slowly leave the University and only the weaker and less courageous would remain. We know that this is the last thing you really want.[224]

This letter was all the more remarkable, as Richard McKeon noted in a confidential advisory to Hutchins, since it manifested the "singular unanimity of a group of men who seldom agree about anything."[225]

---

224. Chester W. Wright et al. to Hutchins, April 9, 1936; H. A. Millis et al. to Hutchins, July 17, 1936, ibid.

225. McKeon to Hutchins, July 29, 1936, Robert M. Hutchins Papers, Addenda, box 92, folder 1.

So disturbed was Frank Knight about the Gideonse case that he drafted a long denunciation of Hutchins's behavior in a seven-page single-spaced letter to Oskar Lange, as a kind of warning about the state of the University when Lange was considering a professorial appointment at Chicago. For Knight the Gideonse case was prime evidence of Hutchins's assault on the local faculty by using a kind of authoritarian medievalism:

> He has only contempt for the opposition, which he treats as either incompetent or selfishly motivated, or both, and he seems to prefer to express this attitude in frankly insulting terms....In so far as he does have any one view, of direction to ride off in, it is pretty clearly the aim of establishing the closest possible imitation of medieval scholasticism. And I am naturally opposed to that. I am especially opposed to it, moreover, because of the individual who would (of course) be Pope. I don't think educational theory in any proper sense is really at issue. It is a question of power.[226]

Lange, who was deeply familiar with the autocratic power of state ministries of education in Europe, must have been mildly amused by Knight's tale of woes, and he assured Knight,

> I am not deterred by it from accepting appointment offered. After my experience with the Polish universities and from what I know about the German universities (I mean here the German universities in pre-Nazi times) such cases as you describe seem only minor blots on a picture which is on the whole clear. The conditions in

226. Knight to Lange, January 14, 1938, Knight Papers, box 60, folder 25.

the Polish universities were such of constant interference, though not from the rectors who have no power, from all possible sides.[227]

Having been rejected for promotion in 1936 and again in 1937, Gideonse decided to publish a scathing critique of Hutchins's various educational essays, especially Hutchins's *The Higher Learning in America*, which had been published in October 1936. Gideonse's final attack came in the aftermath of the controversial attempt of Robert Hutchins and Mortimer Adler to import Scott Buchanan and Stringfellow Barr to create a Committee on the Liberal Arts at the University, whose mandate was (among other things) to think about how a great-books curriculum might be planned at Chicago.[228] Hutchins toyed with the idea of imposing Barr as the new dean of the College, even though he admitted to Adler, "we all know that it is going to be hellish hard to put Winkie [Barr's nickname] over as Dean."[229] These tactics had raised deep opposition in the

227. Lange to Knight, January 30, 1938, ibid.

228. See Adler, *Philosopher at Large*, 172–77. Adler reported to Mark Van Doren in January 1936 that there were "a number of other very definite indications that the College faculty were prepared to fight the President tooth and nail," which, according to Adler, "made Bob so sick at heart that he didn't know what to do.... The reason for the opposition of the College faculty is simple: you guys are somehow related to me and to Bob, and that relation signifies that you are all Catholics, medievalist, scholastics, Aristotelians, and of course sons of bitches, if not of St. Benedict." Adler to Mark Van Doren, January 17, 1936, Adler Papers, box 57. By the summer of 1937 Adler reported: "Chicago is hopeless. From now on, everything will be progressively McKeonized. That's my way of saying that poison is being sprayed on the tree of knowledge." Adler to R. Catesby Taliaferro, July 21, 1937, ibid. See also Amy A. Kass, "Radical Conservatives," 135–55.

229. Hutchins to Adler, September 8, 1936, as well as August 21, 1936, Adler Papers, box 56.

College and in the Division of the Humanities and may have contributed to Richard McKeon's ultimate reservations about Adler's schemes.[230] Gideonse and several others associated with the New Plan curriculum (Coulter, Scott, Schlesinger, Carlson, Keniston, and a few others) tried to produce a collaborative pamphlet critiquing Hutchins's educational ideas as represented in Hutchins's short book on *The Higher Learning in America* in the spring of 1937, but the strategy collapsed when several faculty got cold feet. Gideonse complained to Wirth, "the whole thing made me more sick at heart than anything that has happened this year."[231]

Instead, Harry Gideonse decided to produce his own demarche. In a thirty-four page pamphlet called *The Higher Learning in a Democracy* Gideonse excoriated Hutchins for the latter's call for a new metaphysics that would bring intellectual and moral order to the chaos of American university education, insisting that this was nothing short of imposing an "absolutistic system."[232] Gideonse argued that he was especially troubled

230. See the "Minutes of the Faculty of the Division of the Humanities, May 8, 1937, and October 9, 1937." Hutchins initially sought to have Barr appointed in the College, after vetting by the Department of History. Professor Harley McNair was asked to poll the senior faculty in the department, and he reported that String-fellow Barr was an "exceptionally pleasing person," but also that Barr "makes no pretense of scholarship or scholarly productivity in the sense in which those terms are understood at the University of Chicago." McNair to Brumbaugh, November 26, 1935, Dean of the College Records, 1923–1958, box 2, folder 11.

231. Gideonse to Wirth, April 13, 1937, Louis Wirth Papers, box 4, folder 2. The drafts of several of the chapters are in the Wirth Papers, box 51, folder 1

232. "By constructing a university in this way it can be made intelligible. Metaphysics, the study of first principles pervades the whole....I should insist that a university is concerned with thought and that the collection of information, historical or current, had no place in it except as such data may illustrate or confirm principles or assist in their development." Robert M. Hutchins, *The Higher Learning in America* (New Haven, 1936), 108–9.

by Hutchins's alleged disrespect for modern science: "Acceptance of the curricular primacy of a set of first metaphysical principles would reduce science to dogma and education to indoctrination.…If these are times of confusion and disorder, the results and the methods of science also make them times of unparalleled promise. Now—as never before—educational leadership calls for a persistent and critical emphasis upon the significance of present achievement and its promise for the future."[233] The pamphlet was sufficiently arresting that Hutchins asked Mortimer Adler to comment on it, which he promptly did, but Adler also sent Hutchins a separate letter in which he candidly noted that Gideonse had rich opportunities for intellectual subversion precisely because of Hutchins's imprecise and vague use of words and concepts about "philosophy," "metaphysics," "knowledge of first principles," and the like.[234]

233. Harry D. Gideonse, *The Higher Learning in a Democracy: A Reply to President Hutchins' Critique of the American University* (New York, 1937), 9, 33. Gideonse further elaborated some of his ideas about the importance of educating what he characterized as the "whole man" in "Quality of Teaching or Content of Education?" in *The Preparation and In-Service Training of College Teachers. Proceedings of the Institute for Administrative Officers of Higher Institutions* 10 (1938): 65–75.

234. "As I look back upon the last two or three years of effort in promulgating your educational ideas and policies, I can see the following main errors: (1) that unfortunate distinction between facts and ideas which has been misunderstood, because of the language, on all sides; (2) your use of 'metaphysics' both in place of theory, on the one hand, and in place of philosophy, on the other; and in the connection the very bad phrase 'knowledge of first principles'; (3) the unfortunate phrasing of your attack on 'character training' which has been misunderstood as a failure on your part to take account of the moral virtues in education; (4) the failure to answer the questions, what philosophy or whose metaphysics, which, not satisfactorily answered, leaves everyone with the suspicion that you must absolutely mean Aristotelianism or something like that." Adler to Hutchins, June 25, 1937, Adler Papers, box 56.

Coming from an untenured professor, Gideonse's attack on the president of the University was imprudent, but he may have realized that his chances for tenure at Chicago were already nil. The Department of Economics filed protests with Hutchins, citing Gideonse's extraordinary teaching and his intellectual prowess, but this was to no avail.[235] When Gideonse finally resigned in the spring of 1938 to accept a professorship at Barnard College, Louis Wirth brought an unusual motion before the Faculty of the College, recognizing Gideonse's many talents and contributions and expressing great regret that he was leaving the University community: "His colleagues in the College deeply regret the departure of Mr. Gideonse from the campus of the University of Chicago. Through the many years of labor to establish the present organization, staff, and curriculum, he has generously and devotedly given of his wisdom, his enthusiasm, his energies, and his leadership....We shall long remember with pleasure the democratic and effective manner in which he inspired the loyalty and comradely cooperation of his associates."[236] The motion passed unanimously, with each of the sixty faculty members present rising to signify his or her personal approval. Most problematic was the failure of Aaron J. Brumbaugh, the dean of the College, to support Gideonse strongly and unambiguously, but Brumbaugh was not a distinguished scholar and, in contrast to Boucher, he seemed eager to please

235. H. A. Millis to Hutchins, May 27, 1937, Presidents' Papers 1925–1940, Appointments and Budgets, box 25, folder 10; Millis to Brumbaugh, January 31, 1938, ibid., box 42, folder 10.

236. "Minutes of the Faculty of the College," June 2, 1938, 1.

or at least to accommodate Robert Hutchins.[237] Gideonse's friends clearly felt him to be the victim of a political purge, and Hutchins's obfuscations to student protestors that he had never rejected a recommendation of the deans that Gideonse be promoted, while technically correct (he rejected on several occasions a direct recommendation brought to him by the Department of Economics), sounded slightly threadbare. With Gideonse's departure Hutchins had eliminated a formidable public intellectual with articulate views on liberal education, a man who had the rhetorical skills, the courage, and the capacity for leadership to challenge Hutchins on his own terms.[238] Given that the other senior founding members of the 1931 general-education courses were either disillusioned or distracted and given that the College could only drift with a weak

237. Brumbaugh reviewed the case in January 1938 and after admitting that Gideonse had done an effective job as a teacher remarked, "if the terms of the original agreement [offered to Gideonse by the Department of Economics] were as stated above...it would seem that Mr. Gideonse should either be promoted now or should be given a definite indication as to the chances of his promotion in the near future." See Budget Narrative of the College for 1938–1939, January 29, 1938, Presidents' Papers 1925–1940, Appointments and Budgets, box 42, folders 5–6. Hutchins had little problem ignoring such a "judicious" non-recommendation. Ralph Tyler later remembered that Brumbaugh was "an easy going, nice guy, who could say he believed in all the things Hutchins believed in, but was intellectually, in my opinion, too lazy to think through what that meant and how to do anything about it." Ralph W. Tyler, *Education: Curriculum Development and Evaluation. An Interview Conducted with Malca Chall in 1985, 1986, 1987* (Berkeley, 1987), 160.

238. William Hutchinson noted shrewdly of Gideonse: "Chicago will miss him, although probably Pres. Hutchins isn't sorry to see him go." William T. Hutchinson Diary, entry of May 27, 1938. For Gideonse's later career as an educational leader, see Harry D. Gideonse, *Against the Running Tide: Selected Essays on Education and the Free Society*, ed. Alexander S. Preminger (New York, 1967).

dean in charge of its affairs in the later 1930s, the way slowly opened for the revolution of January 1942.

A radical revisions of the 1930 arrangements, as they related to the relationship between the "Upper" divisions and the College, took place in January 1942. Hutchins's long-term solution to the perceived short-comings of the New Plan was to create a real faculty for the College and to encourage that faculty to develop a full-time, fully required curriculum in general education that would span grades eleven to fourteen for all of its students. Since Hutchins had decided that the real work of the College should begin at the end of the second year of high school and conclude with the second year of the College, he became convinced that the College should exercise its right to hire a separate faculty and that it should gain sole control of the award of the BA degree. Whereas before 1942 the award of the baccalaureate degree had remained a clear divisional prerogative and all members of the College faculty also held membership in the faculty of a division, now the College assembled a faculty larger (on paper at least) than three of the four divisions and it gained control of the baccalaureate degree, creating educational programs that afforded no place for the specialized research knowledge represented by the depart-ments. What had been the "Upper" divisions between 1930 and 1942 now became the "Graduate" divisions that continue to mark the mental and political map of our local academic world. Instead of a BA degree that included both general education and specialized work, the first degree offered by the divisions would now be the MA, with the College's program focusing exclusively on general education. From 1942 the Core, defined by fourteen separate general-education sequences, became the be-all and end-all of an undergraduate education at Chicago.

The logic of the curricular legislation of January 1942, which effec-tively eliminated the departments and their majors from the undergraduate curriculum, was fiercely opposed by many senior faculty members with experiences in the New Plan. For men like Schlesinger, Wirth, and Scott the issue was not, as the proponents of the all-general-education college would later try to argue, of rote memorization in the 1930s survey courses against conceptual learning in the curriculum installed in 1942, since they believed that their work had also encouraged such analytic learning among the New Plan students. Rather, the real division of opinion had most to do with the linkage of general education to more advanced and specialized learning offered by the research faculties in the departments as an integral and necessary component of a baccalaureate degree program, and with the parallel assumption that the faculty who taught general education should have the same kinds of scholarly credentials and career aspirations as those who taught more specialized departmental courses. In contrast to the College curriculum created in 1942 and strengthened in 1946, the New Plan was conceived not as a curricular end unto itself, but as a period of intellectual preparation and transition, leading to the higher and more specialized learning offered in the divisions and the professional schools for the BA or BS degree. Louis Wirth caught this distinction well when he argued in 1937:

> Our conception of a general education is not one separate and distinct from knowledge of any particulars. We hold that we can only have valid general knowledge insofar as we have valid particular knowledge upon which to base it and vice versa....Even in our general education we are not drawing a strict line of separation between knowledge of universals and knowledge of particulars. This intimate interrelationship between general and particular knowledge is all the more evident in our present curriculum beginning upon the termination of the courses given in the College...

We are attempting now in all of the Divisions of the University and all of its Departments to build our curriculum upon what has already been achieved by the student in the College.[239]

The New Plan accomplished this work of translation not only through the structure of its general-education sequences, which embraced the practice of presenting contemporary empirical research in addition to classic texts, but also by offering students in the College the chance to take two specialized sequences as electives in addition to the four general-education survey courses. It was thus understandable that when Hermann Schlesinger criticized the new all-general-education curriculum of 1942, he would focus on the gradual smothering of free electives and the lack of integration within the undergraduate program of general and specialized learning. Schlesinger insisted that the new curriculum

gives the impression of having been designed primarily for students who have developed no individual intellectual interests. In general, those are the students with the least intellectual initiative and the ones least likely to make a real contribution to the life of the nation. I am convinced that the student who has a definite intellectual interest in coming to college will usually be the one who benefits most from his general education. It is this type of student I hope to find in the majority among our future students. But the College will not continue to draw students with intellectual independence if it undertakes a program which throttles individual

239. Louis Wirth, "The University," 5–6, unpublished ms., 1937, Wirth Papers, box 51, folder 1.

talent and curiosity, by prescribing the inflexible program which has been submitted to us.[240]

Similarly, Ronald Crane, who was originally skeptical about the merits of the New Plan, concluded in June 1946 that the all-general-education curriculum adopted in January 1942 was even less attractive:

If the College could get away from the present lock-step system of courses and course examinations, it might be much more easily possible than it is now to interest distinguished scholars or scientists in the Divisions who are also good teachers in College teaching. Everyone recognizes the importance, even for the purpose of general education, of giving College students an opportunity of coming under the influence of such teachers, but it is certain that not many of the more stimulating and original minds in the University would be willing to join the staffs of any of the existing general courses and to teach under the controls involved in their constitution.[241]

Arthur P. Scott kept a private checklist of faculty in the College who overtly or covertly opposed Robert Hutchins's educational ideas, and the names of most of the faculty leaders of the 1931 survey courses were on it, along with Scott himself.[242] It was perhaps noteworthy that the

240. Schlesinger to Clarence Faust, February 10, 1942, Dean of the College Records, 1923–1958, box 21, folder 11.

241. R. S. Crane, "Memorandum on the College Program," 1946, Dean of the College Records, 1923–1958, box 21, folder 12.

242. Arthur P. Scott Papers, box 1, folder 13.

"Memorandum to the Board of Trustees on the State of the University" drafted in April 1944 by Ronald Crane and others, which challenged Hutchins's style of governance as president and his putative revolutionary interest in weakening the power and authority of the departments, was signed by Merle Coulter, Alfred E. Emerson, Ralph W. Gerard, Harvey B. Lemon, Hermann I. Schlesinger, Arthur P. Scott, Louis L. Thurstone, and Louis Wirth, full professors who had played decisive roles in organizing the 1931 general-education curriculum.[243]

In the end, in the struggles between the forces represented by Harry Gideonse and Robert Hutchins we see the collision of two competing curricular revolutions in general education. The one sought to use the most auspicious works of modern social and natural science, grounded in a strong historical and developmental perspective, to imagine a world of general knowledge useful for the active, but highly thoughtful practice of modern citizenship. The other sought to recover from the classic works of the past a more coherent but also more introspective vision of learning, stressing the skills of the individual knower and motivated by active forms of educational connoisseurship. Both constituted vast improvements over the curricular chaos of the 1920s, and both would continue to have powerful resonances in the decades to come, on our campus and in the American academy at large. If mass higher education in the twentieth century was to do more than train the technical and professional elites for their careers, then it would need a cultural and intellectual mission to replace the classical learning of the nineteenth-century curriculum. Growing enrollments, the development of modern science, and the professionalization of scholarship had already killed off the classical

243. A copy of the memorandum is in the Knight Papers, box 60, folder 14, as well as the "Minutes of the University Senate," April 14, 1944.

curriculum. Both Gideonse and Hutchins represented systematic attempts to preserve and to protect the intellectual culture of the modern university against a "collegiate" culture that stressed adolescent amusements more than serious intellectual engagement. The new century needed new alternatives, and the fateful collision of the ideals represented by Gideonse and Hutchins under the aegis of the New Plan made the 1930s a particularly fruitful and memorable time at the University of Chicago.

THE FATE OF THE GENERAL-EDUCATION PROJECT IN THE 1940S

 arry Gideonse believed that the first general-education courses at the University were "an attempt to substitute a twentieth-century cosmos for the almost incredible chaos that has arisen in American higher education as the unplanned fruit of our rebellion against the old classical curriculum."[244] This new cosmos required strong and consistent leadership, but as the 1930s evolved the teams who organized the first general-education courses began to fragment. The first to go was Ferdinand Schevill who left the Humanities course in 1935, following the death of his wife to cancer, and returned to full-time writing. Harry Gideonse was forced out as the leader of the Social Sciences course in the spring of 1938. Louis Wirth and Jerome Kerwin also abandoned the Social Sciences course, although they followed its subsequent history with some

244. Harry D. Gideonse, "Integration of the Social Sciences and the Quest for Certainty," *The Social Studies* 27 (1936): 365.

concern.[245] Harvey Lemon resigned from the chairmanship of the Physical Sciences general course in early 1939. Professional responsibilities had already distracted Hermann Schlesinger who by 1937 was "so busily engaged in other responsibilities that he does not find time any longer to attend regular staff meetings or conferences."[246] To make matters worse, Chauncey Boucher decided to abandon the deanship of the College for the presidency of the University of West Virginia in the spring of 1935. His decision was most likely the result of the embarrassment and frustration that he felt over Hutchins's failure to support the New Plan, and his sense that the attacks in the *Maroon* in the winter and spring of 1934 had Hutchins's good wishes behind them.[247] Boucher had been a strong dean with a clear vision of the kind of educational programs that he thought that the College should pursue and who enjoyed credibility among the faculty. In his place Hutchins appointed Aaron Brumbaugh, a genial administrator and a sometime professor in the

245. Interview of Maynard Krueger with Christopher Kimball, May 25, 1988, 13–18.

246. Lemon to Brumbaugh, November 17, 1937, Dean of the College Records, 1923–1958, box 8, folder 1; Brumbaugh to Lemon and Schlesinger, February 9, 1939, Presidents' Papers, 1925–1940, Appointments and Budgets, box 42, folder 6.

247. After three frustrating years at West Virginia, Boucher was appointed chancellor of the University of Nebraska, where he served from 1938 to 1946. On his later tenure, see Rex J. Cogdill, "A Study of the Chancellorship of Chauncey S. Boucher at the University of Nebraska, 1938–1946" (PhD diss., University of Nebraska, 1995). Ironically, Boucher's relationship with the Nebraska faculty was just as rocky as that of Hutchins at Chicago. A recent study concludes that, in spite of Boucher's many positive accomplishments in running that land-grant university, "his biggest leadership failure appears to be his inability to establish and maintain positive communications with the faculty at Nebraska." Cogdill, 388.

Department of Education who had no serious research credentials and no real educational ideas of his own, and until Clarence Faust's appointment as dean in mid-1941, the College drifted, lacking strong leadership. World War II brought more severe disruptions, and the new all-general-education curriculum that passed in January 1942 and the recentering the BA degree was the final denouement of the New Plan.

The later history of these early "Core" courses was complex, marked in some cases by disillusionment and hurt feelings, but in other cases by remarkable resiliency and great pedagogical progress. The Biological Sciences and Physical Sciences general courses survived into the later 1940s, but the venerable courses were criticized by divisional interests as lacking in sufficient depth to prepare students interested in future advanced study in the sciences. More importantly, they found themselves in serious competition with a set of new Natural Sciences courses developed for the four-year program of the curriculum created in 1942, and they were eventually subsumed into the larger structure of Natural Sciences between 1950 and 1952. The old science courses thus found themselves trapped between new general-education ideals of the post-1942 Hutchins College and the rapidly evolving research professionalism of the post-1945 science establishment at Chicago. Joe Schwab, a forceful leader of the new Natural Sciences program, admitted much later in his life that the competitiveness between the old courses and the new Natural Science courses was by design, since he felt Merle Coulter's course in particular was "very recalcitrant. They had their big package of brittle books and their big package of lectures duplicated for them, and discussions which were nothing but going over those two texts. They were hard. I set up a separate and competitive natural sciences program simply to needle them into change, which it did to about a 25, 30 percent extent."[248] Schwab's assessment of Coulter's course was unduly negative, but it was the case that each group tended to go its own way, the result being that staff members involved in the undergraduate science courses wondered, as they put it in a memo to the dean of the College in 1948, "what the ultimate fate of science in the College was to be. The result [of the competition] was most unfortunate for the College; communication between the staffs broke down almost completely, important educational issues went undiscussed, and personal relations between colleagues were strained."[249]

Still, even within the original Biological Sciences general course one found seeds of change. When Merle Coulter became concerned that the course, in spite of its rhetoric, was emphasizing too much "passive assimilation" of material and too little conceptual thinking about basic biological processes, he commissioned his staff in 1939 to draft a small booklet of "Thought Questions," in which the student encountered two hundred questions that he or she might pose about the material that was being presented, which asked the students "to reorganize that knowledge, to apply it to new situations, and often to add reasoning processes

248. Interview of Joseph J. Schwab with Christopher Kimball, April 8, 1987, 19.

249. Thornton W. Page, J. J. Schwab, H. Vogel, and E. P. Northrup, "A Proposal for the Improvement of the College Programs in the Natural Sciences, confidential [September 1948]," Dean of the College Records, 1923–1958, box 7, folder 6. By 1951 the Natural Sciences staff in the College had abandoned the structure and techniques of the 1931 course, in favor of small sections, meeting five hours a week. See Benson Ginsburg to John O. Hutchens, August 26, 1951, Dean of the College Records, 1923–1958, box 7, folder 7.

of his own in order to arrive at satisfactory answers."[250] Discussion sessions were then formed around the questions, so that students were
forced to think about larger conceptual issues. One of the co-authors of
these "Thought Questions" was the young instructor of biology, Joe
Schwab. Schwab had received his PhB in English literature at Chicago
in 1930 but then shifted to biology for graduate work, receiving his PhD
in zoology in 1938 with a dissertation supervised by Sewell Wright.
Schwab began as a instructor and examiner in the Biological Sciences
general course in 1937 and emerged as an active leader of the College's
all-general-education curriculum after the upheavals of 1942–46. He
later became one of the most famous teachers of the Hutchins College,
but he was also viewed by many colleagues as a partisan of Robert
Hutchins.[251]

Leadership for the Social Sciences general courses after 1938 initially
proved problematic. Once Harry Gideonse left, Aaron Brumbaugh tried
to persuade William T. Hutchinson of the Department of History in
June 1938 to take charge of the courses, offering him both a promotion
to full professor and an increase in salary, but Hutchinson refused to be

250. Merle Coulter, "Report on Ten Years of Experience with the Introductory
General Course in the Biological Sciences," October 1941," 28; M. C. Coulter,
Thought Questions for the Introductory General Course in the Biological Sciences
(Chicago, 1940).

251. Maynard Krueger later recalled that Schwab "had the reputation of not
only being an ardent Hutchins's supporter, he was regarded as a supporter of
everything that Hutchins was suspected of being in favor of, including maybe
some things that Hutchins wasn't in favor of." Interview with Christopher Kimball, May 25, 1988, 22. On Schwab see Donald N. Levine, *Powers of the Mind:
The Reinvention of Liberal Learning in America* (Chicago, 2006), 114–45.

"bogged down" in what he called the "the College morass."[252] A former graduate student of Charles Merriam, Walter H. C. Laves, was then recruited to take charge. Laves valiantly tried to keep the course together between 1938 and 1941, but he was a poor lecturer and lacked Gideonse's wide knowledge of the social sciences.[253] He also lacked the support of his own colleagues, several of whom finally took the extraordinary step of appealing to Hutchins to force Laves out. Under pressure from Hutchins, Laves soon left the University on a leave of absence to work for the government during the war, leaving Maynard Krueger as acting chair of the course.[254]

Some of the early young assistants also turned away. James Cate and S. William Halperin abandoned the College's general-education programs,

252. "I declined promptly because I wish to move into graduate instruction and have more opportunity for research. Thereby I probably missed a full professorship and corresponding advance in salary. But I got out of the College morass of papers, Board of Examiners, etc., 4 or 5 years ago and I'm not prepared to bog down there again, even though by not accepting I sacrifice both money and position." William T. Hutchinson Diary, entry for June 8, 1938.

253. Louis Wirth took Laves's appointment as a signal that "this can mean only one thing, therefore, namely that they are planning not to strengthen but rather to ignore the social science work in the College, hoping probably in that way to put something else in place of it which is more likely to suit the ruling elite." Wirth to Gideonse, July 28, 1938, Wirth Papers, box 4, folder 2.

254. Laves left Chicago in December 1941 to work as a director in the US Office of the Coordinator of Inter-American Affairs. He was soon involved in a number of government jobs, from the Office of Civilian Defense to a consultancy at the Bureau of the Budget, and as an adviser to the US delegation at the San Francisco Conference in 1945 that created the United Nations. Laves became the deputy director general of UNESCO in 1947 and eventually taught at Indiana University from 1954 until his retirement in 1972. He was the first person to hold the Wendell L. Willkie Professorship in Political Science at Indiana.

tempted in the late 1930s by the prestige of departmental teaching and, at least in the case of Cate, disillusioned by Hutchins and with the curricular changes enacted in 1942. Mary Gilson retired from both the Social Sciences general course and the University in 1942, after which she taught at Wellesley College and at Webber College in Florida. Norman Maclean left the Humanities general course in 1937 for full-time teaching in English, but remained active in the affairs of the College, serving as the College's dean of students during World War II. But the cases of Maynard Krueger and Gerhard Meyer demonstrated a positive grafting effect between the earlier and later formats of general education in the Social Sciences. Krueger came to the College (under the formal sponsorship of the Department of Economics) in 1932 from the University of Pennsylvania, having been personally recruited by Harry Gideonse, who knew Krueger from collaborative work they had done together at the University of Geneva in the late 1920s.[255] An ardent socialist, Krueger is best remembered for having run as the vice presidential candidate on the Socialist Party of America's presidential ticket (with Norman Thomas) in 1940. Krueger soon became a fixture in undergraduate social-sciences and economics courses, and was a brilliant teacher. Awarded tenure in 1947, Krueger became in the later 1940s and 1950s an active leader of several of the later Social Sciences Core courses, and in 1958 he was awarded a Quantrell Award for Excellence in Undergraduate Teaching. In May 1937, five years after Krueger had been recruited, Harry Gideonse with the strong endorsement of Louis Wirth successfully proposed the appointment of Gerhard E. O. Meyer as an instructor of Economics in the College, initially as a one-year

255. Interview of Maynard Krueger with Christopher Kimball, April 20, 1988, 25, 43–48; April 28, 1988, 3; H. A. Millis to E. T. Filbey, June 23, 1932, Presidents' Papers, 1925–1940, Appointments and Budgets, box 25, folder 9.

replacement appointment.[256] Meyer was recommended by Wassily Leontief of Harvard, who knew Meyer from having worked with him at the
Institut für Weltwirtschaft in Kiel, Germany, between 1927 and 1929.
A German refugee who was trained as an economist at the University
of Kiel and who worked for one year (1932–33) at the Institut für Sozi-
alforschung in Frankfurt, Meyer fled to Paris in 1933 and ended up
working as a postgraduate student at the University of Manchester in
England from 1935 to 1937.[257] After a rocky start in learning how to lead
discussions, Meyer established a reputation for teaching excellence, and
his probationary appointment was renewed until he was finally awarded
tenure in 1946.[258] Meyer became one of the most beloved faculty teachers

256. See the files in Presidents' Papers, 1925–1940, box 42, folder 1. Hutchins
approved Meyer's appointment for "just one year," but the deadline soon expired
and Meyer was retained. It is not completely clear how Meyer came to Gideonse's attention. It is possible that Leontief at Harvard brought him to the
attention of someone in the Chicago Economics department, such as Frank
Knight, Jacob Viner, Harry A. Millis, or Gideonse himself. Louis Wirth met
with Gerhard Meyer in New York City after Meyer had already visited Chicago,
and wrote to Gideonse, reporting, "I must say [he] impresses me favorably."
Wirth to Gideonse, May 17, 1937, Wirth Papers, box 4, folder 2.

257. The Kiel Institute of World Economics was a remarkable gathering point
of famous and soon-to-be-famous economists in the interwar period, including
Gerhard Colm, Adolph Lowe, Wassily Leontief, Hans Neisser, Jacob Marschak,
and Alfred Kähler. The general orientation of their work was to explore theories
of economic growth and the nature of business cycles from a structural perspective. Several scholars from Kiel ended up as émigrés working at the New School
for Social Research. Gerhard E. O. Meyer had, thus, an excellent scholarly pedi-
gree, even though he ended up publishing very little during his career at
Chicago.

258. "We had some doubts about whether we would get Meyer through [for
tenure]. He didn't have a very good reputation as a conductor of discussion in
what we called Social Sciences I, that later became Social Sciences II. We were
almost at the point where we would have had to send him back to Germany

of the College in the 1950s and 1960s. Ironically, both Krueger and Meyer, who owed their appointments to Harry Gideonse, ended up with what Gideonse most wanted, namely, a tenured appointment on the College faculty.

Moreover, the fate of the Social Sciences course was more congenial and less disruptive than that experienced by the two science courses. Under the leadership of Milton Singer, David Riesman, and Robert Redfield the Social Sciences general course was able to reconstitute itself in the later 1940s as the second in a tier of three year-long sequences, using a framework of two lectures and two discussions per week that enlarged the possibilities of seminar-style discussion in the now much expanded general-education program. In theory, Social Sciences II occupied the functional position enjoyed by the original Social Sciences course. But parts of the original focus of the old course were devolved onto the new Social Sciences I course—particularly the parts relating to the American state and American political culture. After 1947 Social Sciences II focused primarily on culture, personality, and social structure, as it continues to do down to the present day.[259]

when the proposal was made that 'let's try him in the second year course, what later became Social Sciences III, then called Social Sciences II. Let's try him in there.' We shifted him to Social Sciences II and he blossomed out as if he were a new man. Pretty soon he's given the Quantrell award for excellence in undergraduate teaching." Interview of Maynard Krueger with Christopher Kimball, May 25, 1988, 48–49.

259. See David E. Orlinsky, "Chicago General Education in Social Sciences, 1931–92: The Case of Soc 2," in *General Education in the Social Sciences: Centennial Reflections on the College of the University of Chicago*, ed. John J. MacAloon (Chicago, 1992), 115-25, esp. 119.

The Humanities survey course of 1931 was completely transformed in the autumn of 1942, becoming the second part of a multiyear general-education project in the Humanities, and the study of European civilization via the chronological framework of European history was eliminated as the organizing principle of the course.[260] As is well known, however, the study of European history in the College was soon revived as the History of Western Civilization course by a group of young historically minded scholars in 1947, over the opposition of other partisans of the new Hutchins College established in 1942. An unrecognized, but crucial agent in this struggle was Ferdinand Schevill's discussion leader from the 1930s, Norman Maclean. Maclean emerged as a leader of the College faculty during the stormy debates in the spring of 1946 about the fate of the PhB degree, a degree that was the last vestige of the New Plan in that it permitted students some free electives as part of their baccalaureate program. It was largely owing to Maclean's stubborn defense of the importance of teaching European history in the College that the compromise document that was fashioned between the College and the graduate divisions in May 1946 stipulated that the College should create curricular space for a revived history course, which was duly launched as the History of Western Civilization in 1947–48.[261] Maclean believed

260. Neil J. Wilkof, "History and the Grand Design: The Impact of the History of Western Civilization Course on the Curriculum of the University of Chicago" (master's thesis, University of Chicago, 1973), 2, 29–30.

261. See Maclean's defense of the need for a history course in the "Minutes of the Committee on Policy and Personnel," May 13, 1946, 1, and May 16, 1946, 3. Maclean was also at odds with Joe Schwab, whom he accused on May 4, 1946, of "smearing" the colleagues who opposed Schwab's notions about a totally required general-education curriculum. See the "Minutes of the Committee on Policy and Personnel," May 4, 1946, 1.

that "the College should allow for more diversity both in respect for, and in respect to, the complex state of modern knowledge and the variety of interests of students and the Faculty." Among those possible interests he considered the study of history to be "one of the great subjects of a general education, and I would hope it would be represented quantitatively [in the College curriculum] in proportion to its worth and difficulty."[262] Did Maclean do this out of loyalty to Schevill, Scott, Cate, and the other historians with whom he had such profitable and pleasing interactions in the 1930s? If such memories did influence Maclean's staunch leadership, there is a direct human link between the two courses—the Humanities general course from the 1930s and the History of Western Civilization course from the 1950s—centered in the person of the distinguished writer Norman Maclean. Many years later, David Williams, a professor in English in the College and a close friend of Maclean's who had witnessed his political performance during the 1946 debates, would insist simply but categorically, "we owe the History of Western Civilization course to you."[263] Perhaps it was not surprising that Norman Maclean and his friend James Cate emerged in the 1950s, after Hutchins had left Chicago and Lawrence Kimpton led a controversial effort to scale back the curricular claims of the Hutchins College's general-education staffs, as close personal confidants of Kimpton's on the University

262. "The Joint Sub-Committee of the Committee of the Council and the College Committee on Policy and Personnel," May 10, 1946, 4; "The Joint Sub-Committee of the Committee of the Council and the College Committee on Policy and Personnel," May 23, 1946, 6, Dean of the College Records, 1923–1958, box 21, folder 12.

263. Williams to Maclean, April 5, 1966, Maclean Papers, box 18.

faculty.[264] When Kimpton died in October 1977, Norman Maclean gave an eloquent and affectionate eulogy for him.[265]

The staffing of the new discussion-based general-education courses created or recreated in the early and mid-1940s in the Hutchins College was assisted by the integration of teachers from the University High School. A number of secondary school teachers—Robert Keohane, Gladys Campbell, John R. Davey, Howard Hill, Russell Thomas, and Zens Smith were among the most prominent—became involved in the new College-level general-education courses because those courses were now part of an integrated curricular program beginning with grade eleven that comprehended students who in other circumstances would be in their junior and senior year in high school.[266] After the revolution of 1942 some of these individuals became prominent activists on the College faculty, and they contributed substantially to the programmatic élan and high-quality teaching of the Hutchins College, often writing defenses of its logic and practices. They also helped to increase the

264. Kimpton was unusually candid, for example, with James Cate about the (in his view) fear of competition with the departments that continued to animate the stalwarts of the College. He wrote to Cate in 1958: "We are sweating it out slowly on this undergraduate business. Fortunately we allowed an awful lot of time for talk and for changes, and I think the Divisional boys are becoming a little more reassured about the whole situation. The College is getting increasingly worried, and this, it seems to me, is a good thing. Those boys down there really need to be shaken up, and I think we are generating a situation in which precisely that will occur." Kimpton to Cate, May 1, 1958, Cate Papers, box 2.

265. *The University of Chicago Record* 12 (1978): 18–21.

266. See A. J. Brumbaugh to Gladys Campbell, Gertrude Doxey, Howard C. Hill, Robert B. Keohane, and Russell B. Thomas, May 1, 1936, Dean of the College Records, 1923–1958, box 6, folder 4. These individuals were officially transferred to the College staff as of the 1936–37 academic year.

number of College faculty members who did not have divisional appointments: by 1946 less than 20 percent of the faculty of the College had a
joint appointment in a graduate division.[267]

Yet the fact that many of the colleagues appointed to the College
faculty after 1942 were professional pedagogues with a very high level
of teaching competence but not scholars heavily active in traditional
research disciplines highlighted a dilemma that the College would face
for many years to come: if the right kind of teachers were crucial to the
success of the College's general-education courses, who would select
these individuals, and what professional criteria would be used in select-
ing them? In the 1930s the departments had the formal responsibility
for vetting and appointing the instructors who created and sustained
the first general-education courses, and in general, they applied conventional criteria of research promise as well as teaching ability, although
the case of Harry Gideonse himself demonstrated that even a department
with as august a tradition for research productivity as Economics was
prepared to hire a scholar who was very smart, who was a brilliant
teacher, but who had only a modest level of formal publications in his
field. Once the departments were excluded from hiring College faculty,
which happened in 1942, different kinds of criteria were used to hire the
faculty to teach these courses. Harvey Lemon had argued in 1936 that
the future welfare of his particular general-education course would
depend on his ability to hire younger scholars with sound scholarly
credentials, acceptable to the departments as assistant professors, who
would have their primary teaching responsibility in these general-education
courses. If this were not done, "there is grave danger that not only will
the experimental aspects of the enterprise and its continued improvement

267. "Minutes of the Faculty of the College, February 6, 1946," 15.

be lost to sight, but even that the ground already won cannot be attained and consolidated."[268] While Lemon asked the University to commit substantial new resources in the domain of undergraduate teaching, exclusive of graduate education, he was not calling for the creation of a separate College faculty. Yet such a separate faculty was precisely what arrived on the doorstep of the University after 1942, and tensions emerged between the College and the divisions over resources that soon became acute. As Edward Shils would later recall: "There was a condition of beleaguerment. Many of the people in the College felt antagonistic toward the Divisions. Some people because they were excluded; they didn't have appointments in the Divisions....There were a few people who felt that they were fighting against the Divisions....There were a number of people who were at war with the rest of the university, partly because they felt Hutchins was at war and they felt they were protégés of Hutchins."[269] Joe Schwab, from a very different perspective, also remembered a "profound and deep enmity between the entire Collegiate organization and the Departments, the Divisions. They had, after all, lost their hegemony over undergraduates and with it, the hegemony, went part of their budget, a big part. All the undergraduate courses disappeared. There were no longer any 200-courses in the Departments."[270]

268. "The directors of the course should plan ultimately to staff the lectures with men drawn from the discussion section staff of instructors who hold the interest and enthusiasm of this group, advancement to rank to assistant professors should be made as soon as possible in deserving cases; in the meantime advance in salary should be steady." Lemon and Schlesinger, "After Five Years: An Appraisal of the Introductory General Course in the Physical Sciences," 5.

269. Interview of Edward Shils with Christopher Kimball, June 7, 1988, 11–12, 15, Oral History Program.

270. Interview of Joseph J. Schwab with Christopher Kimball, April 7, 1987, 56–57.

The actual number of faculty needed to organize the first general-education courses was small in the 1930s, given the heavy reliance on large lectures as the primary mode of organizing the New Plan courses. Perhaps the most decisive change that accompanied the revolution of 1942 was the slow transformation of our general-education courses from being primarily lecture courses to primarily discussion-based small seminars. This change was salutary for pedagogical reasons, but it required a substantial expansion of instructional personnel. By the early 1950s a significant number of tenured or tenure-track faculty in the arts and sciences had appointments only in the College. As late as 1958, 68 percent (108 of 160) of the faculty with membership in the College had appointments only in the College. With the College having its own faculty, recruited primarily on the basis of teaching ability and curricular imagination and not necessarily high-profile scholarship, it was possible to staff the many sections of the various Core courses with highly motivated and qualified teachers who also had faculty rank. After 1958, when the University abandoned the separate College faculty and adopted the norm that future faculty appointments would be joint with the graduate divisions, the staffing of these many and varied Core sections proved much more challenging.

THE CORE IN
MODERN TIMES

f Robert Hutchins's efforts at a totally general-education curriculum designed for the last two years of high school and the first two years of college offered magnificent claims and impressive accomplishments, they also encountered deep suspicion among several of the divisions and in many of the departments, and, perhaps more importantly, failed to sell itself to the public as a viable alternative in American higher education.[271] When Hutchins left the University in 1951, the College as then constituted lost its most vital patron and protector. Facing serious fears that the applicant base for a grades-eleven-through-fourteen, general-education College was profoundly unsteady (by 1953 enrollments in the College had nose-dived to less than thirteen hundred students), Chancellor Lawrence Kimpton, who as secretary of the Faculties, had sat through and objectively recorded the bitter fights over the curriculum that had transpired in the mid-1940s, decided to launch a counterrevolution. In so doing Kimpton was forced to confront a newly autonomous, relatively large, and deeply resentful group of College-appointed professors who since the late 1940s had come to feel themselves to be a genuine faculty and who acted as such. The result of Kimpton's counterrevolution was the Filbey Report of May 1953 and, subsequently, the Report of the

271. At its high point in the early 1950s the curriculum included fourteen general-education comprehensive exams, including Humanities 1, 2, 3; Social Sciences 1, 2, 3; Natural Sciences 1, 2, 3; History; Foreign Language; Mathematics; English; and OII (Observation, Interpretation, and Integration). The latter course is perhaps the most characteristic symbol of the Faust-Ward College and the one most indebted to the intellectual proclivities of Richard McKeon and his protégés like Joe Schwab.

Executive Committee on Undergraduate Education (ECUE) of April 1958, each of which helped to destroy both the curricular autonomy and, eventually, the autonomous status of the faculty of the Faust-Ward College. The ECUE Report reinstated the idea of departmental majors and specialized study, which perforce meant that the four-year Core of the Hutchins College would have to be scaled back radically to nearly half its original size.

A second rub came when Lawrence Kimpton made the decision in 1953 to begin to recenter the demographic basis of the College from grades eleven through fourteen to grades thirteen through sixteen. In the future the high-school graduate would become the normal, if not exclusive, client of the University's undergraduate programs. Now the crucial question became, to how many years of college study would the normal high-school graduate be held accountable? With College faculty insisting on the necessity of almost three years of general-education course work and the divisions wanting two years of specialized and elective course work, something had to give. In view of that stark fact, compelling the College faculty to accept a two-plus-two structure was a major victory for Kimpton and the divisional forces and a major defeat for the faculty of the College.

The attacks on the Hutchins College in the 1950s produced curricular disarray, resulting in chronic tensions among the faculty as to which of the yearlong Core sequences should survive, and how much space in the new hybrid curriculum that emerged in the late 1950s ought be allocated to general education. These stresses also took their toll on collegial cooperation and on curricular innovation. By September 1962, Dean of the College Alan Simpson was complaining about what he felt to be the College's unsolved problems, including "the rigidity of the general education requirements," "the inadequacy of some upper-class offerings," a "lack of inventiveness in a college which prides itself on being experimental," and "the weaknesses in our appeal to high school graduates—we simply do not attract as broad a band of the best talent or as big a volume of applications as we should." In response Simpson urged that "we ought to face the future on the basis of diversity—in the proportions of general and specialized education required of different students and in the ways in which general education is offered....We can surely safeguard our traditions of general education without insisting any longer that there is only one right plan."[272]

During the 1960s several attempts were made to broker compromises that would restore a unified curriculum, the last one in 1966 essentially giving each of the five new collegiate divisions the right to design its own version of a general-education Core, under which all students were still required to take certain Core courses but were free not to take others. This was a political compromise, not a sound educational program, but it did lower the threshold of conflict and cooled tempers somewhat. It also had the virtue of sustaining a robust, if uncoordinated, set of Core courses in the later 1960s, 1970s, and early 1980s at Chicago at a time when many other American universities were abandoning their general-education programs. To the the extent that Chicago maintained its commitment to general education as a defining principle of liberal education after 1960, a state of affairs that was increasingly rare in American higher education, the "heritage" impact of the continuing Core structures from the 1950s onward cannot be underestimated. [273] The precedent

272. Simpson to the Policy Committee, September 19, 1962, Archive of the College.

273. For the collapse of general education after 1970 see John Guillory, "'Who's Afraid of Marcel Proust?' The Failure of General Education in the American University," and Roger L. Geiger, "Demography and Curriculum: The Humanities in American Higher Education from the 1950s through the 1980s," in

of ongoing structures, even if their future was the subject of intense debate, ensured the survival of general education at Chicago.

Significant change came in 1982 when Donald N. Levine assumed the deanship of the College. Levine set about depriving the collegiate divisions of their separate prerogatives and reassembling a common Core for all students. The result was a new curriculum passed in early 1985, which required the equivalent of twenty-one Core courses out of a total of forty-two courses for a baccalaureate degree. The 1985 reforms created a common curricular platform for all students, thus reestablishing the unity of the Core that defined its original mandate in 1931 and 1942. At the same time these reforms faced three major problems. First, they had the disadvantage of assembling a large general-education component, amounting to 50 percent of a student's total course work in the College, at a period in the University's history when many of the older "College loyalists" on the faculty who were most dedicated to the spirit of the Hutchins Core felt themselves increasingly marginalized. Many newer faculty appointed in the 1970s and 1980s came to Chicago from universities where there was no tradition of general education. While willing to participate in the Core, many of these faculty valued upper-level undergraduate courses in their research specializations as much if not more than Core teaching.

Second, and even more troubling, arts and sciences faculty teaching loads nationally had begun to decline precipitously from those of the pre- and immediate postwar periods.[274] The normal teaching load at

The Humanities and the Dynamic of Inclusion since World War II, ed. David A. Hollinger (Baltimore, 2006), 38–45, 65–66.

274. Jonathan Z. Smith, "Dean's Report to the Faculty of the College," November 25, 1980, Archive of the College. For national trends, see Charles T. Clotfelter, *Buying the Best: Cost Escalation in Elite Higher Education* (Princeton, NJ, 1996), 206.

Chicago had been at least six quarter courses a year as late as the 1950s and 1960s, but by the mid-1980s it had contracted to four courses a year in many Social Sciences and Humanities departments, allocated between graduate and undergraduate teaching. These reductions had an inordinate impact on faculty teaching in the College's general-education programs, leaving College administrators with severe staffing issues for their very large Core curriculum.

A third problem originated in the identity of the Core sequences left over from the Hutchins College. Many of these courses, excellent in their design, were associated with College faculty who had created or sustained them in the 1950s and 1960s. But as new faculty joined Chicago's ranks in the 1970s with joint appointments in both a department and in the College, many were unwilling to participate in older courses over which they had no intellectual control. As the master of the Social Sciences Collegiate Division, Bernard Silberman, put it candidly in 1979,

> the problem would not arise if there was an orderly succession of [Core] courses—old ones dying and new ones emerging in a regular pattern. This doesn't occur. The result is that a course exists that becomes institutionally responsible to a new group of undergraduates but which has relatively little appeal to a new group of social scientists. New recruitment of regular faculty fails since the course in its founding reflected the interests of a small group. Potential new recruits cannot view the course as an accurate reflection of what they do and what they think social science is about.[275]

275. Bernard S. Silberman to the Social Sciences Collegiate Division Governing Committee, May 18, 1979, Archive of the College.

Such critiques did not mean that the general education had lost formal legitimacy, for Chicago was remarkable in not experiencing the curricular meltdown of general-education programs that afflicted many other institutions. But they did signal that if the Core was to survive, it would have to become more flexible and open to intellectual renewal and conceptual revision.

Beginning in the mid-1990s the College embarked on another systematic review of the Core curriculum. This review was informed by a large survey of student opinion on the quality of life in the College, conducted by sociologist Richard Taub in 1995, which found that significant minorities of students were unhappy with the instructional quality of many of the Core sequences, particularly in mathematics and the natural sciences. A second issue in the minds of College leaders was the fact that the 1985 reforms, although of fundamental importance in creating a more coherent curriculum, had sanctioned a very large Core that had the effect of pushing many general-education sequences into the third and even the fourth years of undergraduate study. This pattern contradicted the assumptions of Boucher and the original architects of the Core in the 1930s, namely, that general education should come first, not last, for it prepared younger students for the methods and learning skills necessary for higher-level university work and exposed them to broad areas of knowledge before they were expected to focus on one field of study. The deflection of parts of the Core into the later years of the College made it impossible for students to study abroad in their third year, since many students were forced to spend their junior year taking yearlong general-education sequences that they had been unable to fulfill in the first two years of their studies.

Finally, the debates of the mid-1990s reflected fascinating strains within the faculty themselves about the *relative* importance of the Core compared to other elements of the undergraduate curriculum. The generational changes that Bernard Silberman had pointed out in the late 1970s had grown even more acute in the ensuing decades. In 1990 former Dean of the College Wayne C. Booth, in his role as chair of the Council on Teaching, complained "of the total number of students in the arts and sciences...more than half are undergraduates, but far less than half of faculty teaching time and energy goes into College teaching," fostering a dependence "on altruism and a dwindling tradition of loyalty" to maintain staffing.[276] Two highly respected faculty members in English wrote to the dean of the College in 1996, urging that the Core be shortened to entail fewer requirements and that more room be made for students to choose their own programs of study. These steps would create "stronger majors...that would include more faculty advising and more extracurricular contact between students and faculty," along with "a broader menu of the kinds of classes undergraduates take, ranging from large lectures to intimate junior and senior seminars" and "significantly higher stipends for graduate students coupled with significantly more teaching."[277] Their views were quietly shared by many other faculty across the four divisions. Faculty opinion on the size of the Core was all over the map, with older faculty, particularly those with personal connections to the Hutchins College era, attached to the idea of a very large Core, but many younger faculty impatient with (what they felt to be) its virtual domination of the undergraduate experience.

By the autumn of 1997, after a set of often contentious debates involving many dozens of faculty members, a plan emerged that would reduce

276. "Minutes of the Council of the Senate," November 13, 1990, 6.

277. Memorandum of Bill Brown and Miriam Hansen to John W. Boyer, August 1996, Archive of the College.

the size of the Core by several courses (from twenty-one to eighteen or even fifteen, depending on how a student met the foreign language requirement), substituting two-quarter Core courses—designated "doublets" by the master of the Physical Sciences Collegiate Division at the time, Sidney Nagel—in place of yearlong sequences in the biological sciences, humanities, civilizational studies, and the physical sciences. The plan was intended to allow most students to complete their Core requirements in the first two years of study, while also increasing the number of free electives to allow third- and fourth-year students greater freedom to explore advanced courses taught by regular faculty that were open to undergraduates and offered not only in the departments but in several of the professional schools. The scheme also rejected any attempt by the departments to cull more courses to add to their majors. Instead of a curriculum dominated by the Core, general education now assumed the role of a third of a student's curricular plans, similar to the share of Core courses required by Boucher's New Plan curriculum of 1931. The doublet model was structured to allow for more experimentation and for the development of new options in the Core curriculum, thus addressing the problem of frozen-up courses to which Silberman had alluded twenty years earlier.

The logic of the proposal was based on the belief that a slightly smaller, but more intensively focused and organized general-education curriculum would still serve the original functions of the Core with which Chauncey Boucher had first endowed it in 1930, namely, to recruit students who are more academically oriented and to give them an intense synoptic intellectual experience that would introduce them to the broader scholarly values of the University during their first two years on campus. The primary purpose of the reform was to ensure the long-term survival of the Core by returning it closer to the size that it had originally enjoyed in the 1930s, while also opening it up to new intellectual impulses and scholarly movements. Given that Chicago's quarter system functioned, in terms of the typical workload imposed on College students, almost like semesters in other top colleges, the defenders of the plan believed that there would be no net loss of intellectual "intensity" in the College. Indeed, to the extent that the new curriculum allowed students to take more graduate-level courses as free electives, the result might even be a bolstering of the College's famed academic rigor.

The College Council passed this plan in March 1998 by a vote of 24 to 8. The new curriculum went into effect in the autumn of 1999, with current students being given the option in March 1999 to opt to conclude their studies under the old (1984) or the new (1999) Core curriculum. About 95 percent opted to join the new curriculum immediately. While the vote was legitimate, the outcome did not sit well with some senior faculty, who believed that the central administration had somehow forced the changes in the name of creating a "Chicago-lite" experience that would enable the admissions office to attract more applicants who would be inclined to work with less rigor in the College. It was perhaps inevitable that the size and structure of the Core would become intertwined with another contentious issue—the size of the College's student population—in the minds of faculty and alumni in polemical and controversial ways in 1997 and 1998. Both issues became flash points for critics, who believed that the plans for the College repudiated a hallowed and sacred past. Thanks to the aura of a distantly remembered Hutchins (who had now been absent from campus long enough to be embraced, even by those who did not particularly like undergraduates) and the traditions of the Core, Chicago seemed to these critics to have a stronger tie to a shared, cultural patrimony than other universities. The impatience of younger faculty with fixed canonical texts, the desire of many to trim Core requirements, and the appearance of new options of advanced study (like theater and performance studies, cinema studies, gender and sexuality studies, race studies, and environmental studies) appeared to signify an ominous threat to older traditions.

Yet the two decades since these changes have proven such fears groundless, as demographic and curricular developments have produced a College that is more rigorous and just as reverent to its unique educational traditions and to the Core. The more than six thousand undergraduates who will matriculate in autumn 2017 are more talented and intellectually ambitious and better prepared for the challenges of our curriculum than any in our history. The Core curriculum itself continues to offer a series of intellectually exciting and rigorous two- and three-quarter sequences, some dating back to the 1990s but many others created in the past twenty years under new faculty leadership. Indeed, what has been especially gratifying to observe is that interest in and commitment to the Core is significantly higher and more intense among the faculty than it was twenty years earlier. We know that the continuity, vitality, and discipline of the Core curriculum is a powerful attraction for our students, who are now making the University of Chicago their first choice in numbers that would have seemed unlikely even ten years ago. The ten new majors approved in the College since 1997—most recently creative writing and astronomy and astrophysics—have similarly been designed and operationalized with the same rigor and seriousness of intellectual engagement with ideas and evidence that characterized the New Plan.

Jerome C. Kerwin, Moffett Studio, Chicago, January 16, 1947

TRACES AND
MEMORIES

oday we seek to protect the ideal of the scholar-teacher, men and women of distinguished scholarly attainments who teach a range of specialized courses on the upper-undergraduate and graduate levels, who also maintain a serious dedication to the idea of collaboratively taught general-education courses. In this specific sense, we have returned to the operational ideals of the New Plan of the 1930s, while retaining the general-education model of small discussion groups favored by the 1950s. Carl R. Moore, the distinguished endocrinologist and chair of the Department of Zoology put the issue well in 1935: "there seems preponderant evidence of a fairly high correlation between these two types of scholarly activity [teaching and research] at the college level which leads to the conclusion that the University should be and can be staffed at all levels by creative scholars who are also selected and rewarded for being excellent teachers."[278] As I look at the faculty of the College today, I see many such colleagues, and they are the best hope that the traditions launched ninety years ago will continue to flourish in this century.

Yet the history of the early general-education courses reveals how fragile the enterprise of collectively taught courses is, how dependent they are on a small group of leaders and on imagination, and, equally noteworthy, how critical the support of the University at large and especially of the central administration is to sustain these programs. Ironically, in its collective portrait of itself to the wider public the University of Chicago has naturalized the tradition of general education,

278. Carl R. Moore to Brumbaugh, December 10, 1935, Dean of the College Records, 1923–1958, box 6, folder 10.

but our community has not always recognized how challenging it is to sustain the quality and the integrity of these courses. For our traditions to flourish, each generation of faculty must embrace Chicago's general-education tradition as one of the University's highest educational priorities. Accordingly, the College has over the past twenty-five years cooperated closely with the graduate divisions and the departments in articulating the ideal of the scholar-teacher as the norm for faculty appointments. This means that we insist upon both distinguished research work *and* a dedication to high-quality teaching on all levels, including in the Core.

The first general-education courses established the principle that it was beneficial to our students for faculty to collaborate and plan multi-quarter sequences, rather than simply offering whatever might be convenient for or of personal interest to individual faculty members. We placed the educational needs of our younger students in the foreground, and since the 1930s they have never left the spotlight of our College. The New Plan also created strong possibilities for educational innovation, what David Riesman once called "stirring the pot."[279] Regular curricular deliberations in the general-education staffs and the coming and going of faculty teachers over the decades created expectations that there are always better ways of thinking about given pedagogical and substantive issues, and new faculty joining the general-education staffs were encouraged to embrace this kind of ferment. Chauncey Boucher was particularly proud of the fact that the printed syllabi for the four general-education courses were reworked and revised each year, thus

279. Riesman to Milton Singer, December 20, 1947, Dean of the College Records, 1923–1958, box 8, folder 3.

giving the teachers of the courses regular opportunities for experimentation and innovation.[280]

With the exception of Harry Gideonse, the first Core courses were uniformly products of Chicago faculty intramuralism, developed by faculty with long connections to the institution and who were respected by their departmental colleagues. (Merle Coulter, Harvey Lemon, Hermann Schlesinger, and Louis Wirth had received both their undergraduate and doctoral degrees at Chicago, while Arthur Scott received his doctorate on the Midway. Although educated elsewhere, Ferdinand Schevill and Jerome Kerwin had been on the faculty for many years before the new general-education courses were launched in 1931.) The "fit" between the culture of the University faculty and the new educational structures of the College was thus cushioned and empowered by the fact that the leaders of the new courses had solid records of trust and reliability among their colleagues. This may be one reason why the creation of general education at Chicago was able to engender two special attributes among our students that were clearly of immense value to the faculty. The first was serious intellectual engagement by undergraduate students with a challenging, common program of study. The devotion of our students to intense and thought-provoking forms of learning in their first two years at the University was encouraged by the excitement and the imagination of the first general-education courses. In the New Plan our students encountered and profited from the faculty's own intellectual virtues and gained thereby an appreciation of the enthusiasm, but also the seriousness of intellectual engagement. Over the decades since 1931 the intellectual seriousness of our undergraduates has marked the University as a singular place in the world of American higher education.

280. Boucher, *The Chicago College Plan*, 40–41.

A second crucial characteristic of our culture that owes much to the Core is academic freedom. The University of Chicago endured several disagreeable crises in the twentieth century to defend the academic freedom of faculty and students alike, and it is no exaggeration that we became a model for other universities, giving them courage to stand up for their rights as well. As one trustee put in it in 1935, in the wake of the Walgreen fiasco, "I have thought a great deal about the University of Chicago and the difficulties which you are now passing through. I believe that we are making history in our stand for academic freedom and that we will all realize after the storm has blown over, how wise we were in not yielding to the emotional pressure of the moment."[281] Yet the capacity of the University to sustain true academic freedom has hinged on our ability to teach our youngest students from the very beginning of their academic careers at Chicago the importance of the reasoned understanding of conflicting positions, the need for rigorous interrogation of rival claims, and the value of action that is informed by thoughtful reflection. Our general-education courses have come to serve as sturdy launching points for such exemplary teaching. Without an undergraduate student body that accepts the robust practice of academic freedom, the University's ability as a community to sustain such controversial traditions would have been severely impeded.

Both of these concepts—intellectual seriousness and academic freedom—have defined the basic mission of our University, which is to sponsor the creation, the preservation, and the transmission of knowledge, and both concepts were profoundly enhanced in the 1930s by the pedagogical culture that our general-education courses helped to create

281. Albert L. Scott to Harold H. Swift, May 9, 1935, Harold Swift Papers, box 190, folder 4.

and sustain. In challenging our students to engage large areas of human knowledge and discovery, and to do so at a high level at the beginning of their careers, general education contributed to the intellectual serious-ness with which we endow the whole of our curriculum. And in teaching students how to differentiate good from bad ideas, sound from faulty reasoning, and precise from imprecise arguments, general education has had a powerful seeding effect in training generations of young under-graduates in the skills of the scholar: intellectual engagement, dispassion in the midst of controversy, and courage in the face of intellectual uncertainty.

The general-education programs of the 1930s were born in the heat of intellectual controversy based on conflicting modes of scholarly inquiry. The founders of these courses did not intend that their content should be unchanging, for to view them in such a light would have turned them into mausoleums, not exciting educational projects. The notion that Chicago's general-education traditions have always been or should be always be fixed is not only unhistorical, it also violates the very premises on which the New Plan was founded. The architects of the New Plan knew that our general-education programs must be dynamic, or they would fail to engage the imagination of faculty and students of the future.

The New Plan also enabled remarkable efforts to think about the sequencing of collegiate learning in a major research university and about how liberal learning in the College might be connected with under-graduate education in the professional schools. The existence of undergraduate business, law, and social-work programs in the 1930s, based on the foundation of the New Plan's general-education courses, gave interested College students a number of flexible opportunities to connect general and professional education. That the University of Chicago throughout the life of the New Plan had an undergraduate business major, undergraduate degree programs in the School of Social Service Administration and the Divinity School, and a program that was tantamount to an undergraduate law major demonstrate the curricular robustness and the capacity for living with both irony and complexity that marked the University's engagement with undergraduate liberal education in the 1930s and 1940s. The Professional Option program for Chicago undergraduate students interested in careers in business that was authorized by the College and the Graduate School of Business in 1953 and that operated effectively until the early 1990s was a direct descendant of these pre-1942 partnerships between liberal and professional education. The Chicago Careers in Business program, created jointly by the College and the Booth School of Business in 2006–7 and recently named in honor of Byron D. Trott, is the latest iteration of a collaboration that now extends back over a century.

Finally, the general-education structures of the 1930s encouraged the loyalty of brilliant teachers, and such serious dedication to teaching on the part of the faculty became a longstanding component of the College's faculty culture. In 1942 a middle-aged German refugee from Frankfurt, Germany, who was seeking employment as a secondary schoolteacher wrote to a school principal in Massachusetts with his views as to the value of studying history. Trained as a classical historian at the University of Frankfurt, Christian Mackauer argued that more than anything else the study of history should not be a mobilization of ideas or facts presented in predigested formats, but rather that teachers were dealing with "the souls and minds of boys and girls. The different courses of the curriculum are as many different sets of gymnastic apparatuses for the development of intellect, judgment, character of the young people entrusted to your care." Mackauer went on to argue:

It will be an immense service to the student when he learns to see clearer and clearer the deepest foundations upon which he rests his judgments, often without knowing it. The discussion of historical problems may help him to discover inconsistencies in his opinions, logical mistakes in his way of reasoning, or gaps in his factual knowledge; but it will never irreverently touch his genuine last convictions. The consciousness that sincere differences of attitude among members of one nation exist and are to be respected will be one of the most valuable results of this kind of education through History.[282]

Embedded within the semantic structures of Mackauer's arguments were profoundly value-laden remnants of European culture. For Mackauer was above all interested in defending the freedom of the individual mind, which, in his view, could only be protected by being forced to engage in intellectual activities, much as a professional gymnast exercises to attain a kind of freedom with his body. Mackauer was no less committed to the cultural and ethical values of European civilization than Ferdinand Schevill, but Mackauer was writing at a time and was a member of a generation that could no longer ignore or dodge the central issue of individual pedagogical agency for the student himself. Schevill believed that studying European culture would reveal to his students the complexities of their civilizational heritage, whereas Mackauer insisted that

282. Mackauer to David R. Porter, headmaster of Mount Hermon School, August 22, 1942, Christian Mackauer File, Faculty and Staff Files, Mount Hermon School, 1881–1971, Archives of the Northfield Mount Hermon School, Massachusetts. Having been fired from his position as a Gymnasium teacher in 1937 because his wife was Jewish, Mackauer fled Germany in 1939 for Great Britain. He immigrated to the United States in June 1940.

this heritage had to be treated as an intellectual problem to begin with, to be puzzled over, to be understood in its utter complexity, for the good of the development of that ideal of individual freedom that Schevill had postulated as originating within the European tradition. For Mackauer, studying freedom was not enough. One must practice being intellectually free, and this could happen only through the active involvement of the student in the mechanisms of learning. Ferdinand Schevill may have been a hostage of the First World War, but Christian Mackauer was a hostage of the Second.

Christian Mackauer's eloquent prescriptions offered a fitting transition to the College of the later 1940s and indeed to our time as well. When he wrote this letter, Mackauer knew little or nothing about the general-education traditions of our College. He would eventually have a rich field of opportunity to apply and to realize them when he became a central actor in the creation of the new History of Western Civilization course in the College after 1948. But the sentiments that Mackauer expressed would have been most congenial to the men and women who organized and then defended the educational program of the New Plan. Mackauer was a fitting successor to Ferdinand Schevill in his estimation of the immense importance of the European tradition for American intellectual and cultural life. But he was also an institutional heir of Harry Gideonse, for like Gideonse, Mackauer believed that students had to comprehend the complexity and even arbitrariness of received ideas in order to understand their own possible roles in modern society. Moreover, it was deeply fitting that Christian Mackauer was first hired at Chicago in October 1943 not to teach Western Civilization, which did not yet exist, but to teach in the Social Sciences general courses by Maynard Krueger and Gerhard Meyer, who themselves had been hired by Harry Gideonse in the 1930s for the New Plan courses designed by

Wirth, Kerwin, and himself.[283] This lineage of talent and conviction was both durable and remarkable.

The general-education tradition at Chicago that Christian Mackauer embraced in the autumn of 1943 was of fundamental importance in reaffirming the basic culture of the University. Perhaps more than any other leading private American research university, the academic culture of our students and the academic culture of our faculty at the University of Chicago substantially overlap, and this shared culture, in turn, provides for a common intellectual citizenship among students and faculty alike. As the revolutionaries of the 1930s clearly understood, the existence of and operational impact of the new general-education sequences was a primary motor in encouraging and sustaining an intense academic enthusiasm among our students.

Without the project of general education the University would not only have been educationally poorer, it would be culturally a very different place for faculty as well as for students. The launching of general education ninety years ago indeed signified, as Harry Gideonse insisted, the creation of a new cosmos for the University of Chicago.

283. Mackauer was initially hired late in the appointment cycle of the 1943–44 academic year as a one-year visiting instructor to teach Social Sciences, while on a leave of absence from the Mount Hermon School. See Faust to Filbey, November 3, 1943, Presidents' Papers, Addenda, Budgets and Appointments, 1938–1945, box 2, folder 32. Given that the College was recruiting other teachers from elite private high schools—Eugene Northrop in Mathematics was recruited from the Hotchkiss Academy in 1943, for example—Mackauer's appointment made sense and was part of the rapid expansion of the College's faculty that took place after 1942.